A Tale

of the

Ozarks

Donald E. Posten

Ralph and Velma Clark Posten
Some of Their Kin
And Their Times

TABLE OF CONTENTS

PREFACE

THIS IS THE story of a family who, starting in the middle of the nineteenth century, made their home in the Missouri Ozarks, primarily in Pulaski County. The tale begins with a wedding in 1939, jumps back into various periods of history, and ends with the death of the same two people featured in the wedding, Ralph and Velma Clark Posten.

What follows will not please any reader who is seeking a dedicated family tree that carefully traces family origins across the centuries. The reader will find some of that: dates of births, marriages, deaths. But my primary interest has been to learn what I can about the actual lives of the people in this story.

My choice of subjects is random, leaning to life stories that caught my interest, or, frankly, people about whom I either had or could find more information. There was much to learn. Jabez Abel Bostwick is a distant relative, connected through Phoebe Posten Bostwick. He was, after all, an individual of considerable prominence as a cofounder of Standard Oil, and yet I had never heard of him. John Ewing, a captive of the Indians, related through Nora Clark Daily, was another interesting character, but again, I had never heard his name mentioned. It never occurred to me, previous to starting this project, that there is a house in Delhi, New York, which was owned and lived in by one of my ancestors and is now on the National Register of Historic Places. On the other hand, Benjamin Avery Posten and Mary Ellen Dean were familiar names, but there was much to learn as I looked more closely at their lives, and especially into their correspondence.

The voices of memory are also a good source of information, and I especially thank my siblings, Eddie, Cora, Carl, and David for their contributions regarding our parents and grandparents.

In addition to learning about these individuals through their letters, journals, and other unpublished works, it has been helpful to review books, newspapers, and other published information sources that speak to the cultural and historical background of the times and places where they lived.

It is common knowledge that all of us, including the subjects of this writing, tend to understand the world and hold beliefs that are strongly formed by the family and community of which we are part, and by the generation in which we were born.

One generation may perceive the manners, ideas, or ways of living of past generations as primitive. Alternatively, one might view the past with a nostalgic glow, imagining that that manner of life was superior to the present. It is not my intention to promote either concept.

These were simply lives that were lived, and are no longer. Their perceived faults or admirable traits all get meshed together in time. They pass before our eyes like images on a screen. There are characters, roles, plots, and eventually tentative conclusions. But, as in a serial drama, one conclusion merely leads to another episode and often evolves into the introduction of yet another character, in a never-ending story.

All the characters in this story lived complicated lives. The brief sketches provided here belie that complexity. There is far more to the story than revealed or known here. There are even other versions of the truth. The whole truth of each life is something only the one who lived it could reveal, were they here to speak for themselves.

The ancestry of any family is a complex matter, involving multiple marriages throughout the generations, with the resulting intermix of ethnicity, culture, and social mores. Simply stated, this writing does not attempt to be a history, but rather a story. Many stories, or tales really, manufactured from bits and pieces of information. It is one person's rendition of how some of these pieces fit together, or, in some instances, is simply the telling of an interesting story. At times I have taken the best information available and connected the dots using a little imagination.

In excerpts of actual correspondence I have not attempted to correct spelling, grammar, or punctuation, but have presented the material as it was written.

Although this is neither an academic work nor an attempt to create a systematic history of the subjects involved, many sources were consulted from which much information has been drawn. A list of these sources can be found at the end of this book.

In sum, the depiction of events and personalities in this book are of my own making, and I alone bear responsibility.

DEDICATION

This book is dedicated to the memory of Ralph and Velma Clark Posten.

1939: A WEDDING IN RICHLAND, MISSOURI

A BRIEF ITEM in the *Richland Mirror* told of the marriage of Ralph Posten and Velma Clark on March 17, 1939.

The wedding was a small, simple affair, occurring not in a church, but rather in the living room of a minister, Reverend Ben Kissinger. The others in attendance were Verga, Velma's twin sister, and her husband, Glenis, both of whom served as witnesses.

The choice of witnesses was largely Velma's doing. Although Verga had married earlier, the twins remained close, and there was no one Velma trusted more. The wedding announcement in the paper noted that the couple had already made plans to move to California.

Great events were happening in the world in 1939, most of which were worrisome. Hitler was busy advancing the Third Reich, making plans for more war, invading Poland in September. The United Kingdom declared war on Germany. The United States, as well as much of the world, was still suffering from the Great Depression.

Momentarily the war in Europe was of less importance to the couple than their nuptials, but the local economy was very much on their minds. The Depression was easing as economic recovery slowly took place, but conditions in the Ozarks were still bad. Unemployment was high. Jobs were hard to come by and wages were low. In the month the couple was married, the *Richland Mirror* advertised a 1939 Ford VH Coupe for $584, and a room at the Richland Hotel could be had for as little as one dollar a night. Gasoline may have been only nineteen cents a gallon, but that made little difference if the minimum wage was only thirty cents an hour, and even those jobs were often difficult to score.

The year 1939 was also a great year for movies that were to become classics. *Gone with the Wind, The Wizard of Oz,* and *Stagecoach* all appeared on the big screen. It is not known whether Ralph and Velma saw any of these films that year, and they certainly could not afford a new car. But their outlook on the world, despite all the obstacles, was brighter. Dreaming of a better life in California had already begun. They were not just getting married, they were moving on, getting out. Goodbye to the farm, farewell to the harsh economic conditions of the Ozarks, and off to the Golden West to pursue their own dreams. Many of their relatives had already gone that direction, and the young couple anticipated joining them in their own adventure.

The union of Ralph and Velma that March day would bring together several family surnames, along with the lives attached to that history. From Velma came the Clarks, originally from England and then New York State. Nora, Velma's mother, provided the link with the Daily and Burris names, both houses of English and Irish origin. The Postens came from Germanic lands, and arrived in the Ozarks after years in Pennsylvania, their journey halted by the Civil War. Ralph's mother, Phoebe, brought along the Cruikshanks from Scotland, and the Bostwicks, who started out in England and were among the very early American settlers.

THE CLARKS

THE CLARK FAMILY arrived in Pulaski County in the Ozarks in 1891, some twenty years after the Postens homesteaded in the same area. That story will be told later.

The Clarks moved from New York State by train. They had carefully planned for this move, and it was a big one. Three generations were to make the journey, and some relatives were likely already in Missouri. Carl Clark, who would later become Velma's father, was only one year old at the time. He was accompanied by his parents, Luverne and Belle Clark; three other siblings, Myrl, Mable, and Beulah; and his grandparents, Lewis and Mary Clark. Luverne's brother, Verette, also came to Missouri.

By the turn of the century the family had been in Missouri nine years. Luverne and Belle had added four additional children: Grace, Earl, Dewey, and Alta. Ruby would arrive later.

Carl and his parents had been born in New York, as had many other ancestors. One, Icabod Clark, had served as a private in the Revolutionary War.

The reasons a family so long established on the East Coast had for moving to rural Missouri can only be guessed. Perhaps they relished the idea of moving to an area less populated than their native state. It is possible the low cost of land enticed them. It may even be that things were not going well in New York, but there is no record that indicates such. Whatever the Clarks' reasons, Pulaski County was very much in the backwoods and far from their home. While they all had farming backgrounds, they had also lived and moved in more populated areas, had even likely visited New York City. They knew what modern looked like, and it was clearly not to be found in 1891 rural Pulaski County.

One thing seems certain: the Clarks knew what they were getting into. They were anything but impulsive. Smart, practical, and calculating, they had carefully considered all the ramifications of this major transition. In 1891 Missouri was a long journey from New York. Traveling by train was definitely easier than over land by wagon, as earlier settlers from the East would have done. Furthermore, they came with all their belongings, renting several boxcars to move furniture, farm implements, and animals. After evaluating all considerations, they sold their land in New York while making plans to settle in Missouri.

As a point of reference, Francis Parkman took off on the Oregon trail in 1846 and later wrote a book about his experience.[1] Parkman surmised that people took such arduous journeys—leaving their homes and neighbors and uprooting their lives to go to unknown places—for a variety of reasons that ranged from desire for change and escape from an unhappy life to simply having an adventure. He observed that regardless of their reasons, most people, once their destinations were reached, were less than pleased and ready to move on if the opportunity presented itself.

There is no record of the Clarks having any regrets, and if they had they would not have put much energy into them. The

Missouri Ozarks had become their home, a new root, a place to live out their lives. The fact that the Clarks had lived for many years in the East did mean that aspects of their language, idioms, and habits were different from their new neighbors'. One older Pulaski County resident remembered that when the Clarks first arrived, even their manner of dress was more sophisticated than the locals.

The Clarks adjusted to the new location. Although they lived on a farm, they could travel by horse and wagon to Richland and Waynesville. Thanks to the railroad, Richland of 1891 was a bustling town that hosted a local thriving marketplace. There was a general merchandise store, a restaurant, a livery business, a millinery, a blacksmith, a marbleworks, and shippers of stock, produce, and grain. There were real estate and insurance agents, a photographer, a barber, a jeweler, a shoe shop, and a harness shop, as well as two hotels. All this and the railroad itself made the town a center of activity.[2]

It was definitely not New York City, but in Missouri, in the Ozarks, in Pulaski County circa 1891, Richland was clearly the place to be.

CLARKS IN AMERICA

CARL CLARK'S DIRECT ancestors can easily be traced to John Clark, who was born about 1740 in Westchester County, New York. One son was named Ichabod (1766–1840), whose son Gilbert (1790–1852) was the father of Lewis Henry Clark (1836–1920), who in turn was the father of Luverne DeForest Clark (1863–1947). And Luverne was the father of Carl (1890–1977), Velma Clark's father.

There were many Clarks in America. Writer Edgar Clark wrote a history of one Samuel Clark, who was born in Plymouth, a city on the south coast of Devon, England, and emigrated to America in 1636. Huntington's *History of Stamford, Connecticut* gives further details about this man, naming Samuel as one of about twenty men who originally settled Stamford, Connecticut.[3]

One of Samuel's sons, William Clark Sr., went on to become one of the founders of another city in December of 1680. William, along with fifteen others, purchased from Native Americans the land that was later to be known as Bedford, New York. That town was burned by the British during the Revolutionary War and was later rebuilt. The connection with the Clarks of Pulaski County is unclear, but a number of Carl Clark's relatives, including Gilbert and Ichabod, listed Bedford as their place of birth.

Writer Edgar Clark declared after completing his own research that there were so many families named Clark who settled in the Connecticut Valley between 1631 and 1636 that it is difficult to tell just who is related to whom.

Devon, also known as Devonshire, is the English county that was the ancient home of the Clarks. Writer Edgar Clark provides an insightful quote from one family researcher who visited that county investigating the Clark history:

> The Clarks have never been an uppish, pretentious people; most of them farmers, plain, simple, honest people, always well enough in a worldly sense to show them capable of caring for themselves without mean occupations and poor enough to show they are not grabbers of everything in sight, and with too much love for freedom to be sycophants or royal favorites.[4]

Although written many years previous to the time of the Clarks of the Missouri Ozarks, the remark could well describe them. Hardworking, humble, and neither expecting nor requesting help outside what they themselves could provide.

CLARKS IN THE OZARKS

AFTER SETTLING IN Missouri, Luverne and Belle built a fine white two-story house with large rooms. They needed plenty of room, as they came to have nine children and probably housed some of their extended family as well. Likely residents include Lewis Clark and Mary Elizabeth Starr, Carl's grandparents. Mary Starr's first ancestor in America was Thomas Starr, who was born in Kent, England, in 1567 and arrived in America in 1637; he died in Massachusetts only three years after his arrival. As previously noted, Lewis was born to Gilbert and Polly Snider Clark. When Mary Starr died in 1907, Lewis went to live with Verette, one of his other sons living in Missouri.

Luverne and his sons farmed the land as their ancestors had, and from all appearances, the family acclimated well enough to their new surroundings and made friends in the community.

Neighbor and diarist Robert Lincoln Barlow observed on January 1, 1901, that Carl Clark, then around ten years of age, had come home with Barlow's son, Roscoe. More than a week later, on January 11, he noted that several people in the community were ill, including "Mr. Clark," a reference to either Luverne or his father, Lewis.[5]

In 1930, after more than forty years in the Ozarks, Belle

died. Alta Belle, Luverne and Belle's unmarried daughter who lived at home, took up housekeeping duties and caring for her father. She was said to have had a great love of flowers and plants. She died in May of 1935 of measles, the same disease that took her brother Earl in 1934. The obituary noted that just before her death, "She had visions of her heavenly home and joyfully proclaimed the beauties therein."

After Carl and Nora Daily were married, they built a house less than a mile from Carl's parents' farm. They lived there until late in their lives and it was the home of their daughter Velma throughout most of her youth. After Carl and Nora left the farm, the house was eventually sold to a neighbor and later completely remodeled by David Posten.

The original house consisted of a large kitchen, dining room, living room, and one large bedroom. Above the lower level was a large attic, which served as the bedroom for all five of the Clark children. There were porches both front and rear. The front porch featured a bench swing that was frequently in use. A large wood stove commanded a prominent place in the dining room and provided sufficient heat for the entire house. Carl Clark was known for keeping a warm house and a huge stock of seasoned firewood outside, ready for anything winter might bring.

Carl was concerned about tornadoes, and had good reason to be; a storm had once struck a neighboring farm. The house had no basement, so Carl built a crude shelter in an adjoining field. The underground storm shelter was supported by timbers and had a dirt floor; not very inviting, but it would provide shelter from a storm.

The Clarks were frugal. There was not a lot of money in the

first place, and what they did spend tended to go toward some practical benefit. Carl had been a lifelong farmer, although for a time in 1914 he worked in St. Louis on a streetcar. A picture postcard sent in July 1914 to his brother Myrl, who was still back on his own farm in the Ozarks, contained a brief message:

> *Dear Bro. Did you have a fine rain. It sure is warm in St.L.*
> *I got me a job. O.K. It is a fine job. Ans soon. Your bro*
> *Carl Clark.*

The twenty-four-year-old young man had ventured off to the big city and found a job he liked. He'd been married to Nora since 1911. Had he been seeking a life outside the farm? Whatever his reasons for locating in St. Louis, his message to his brother did not mention Nora or Cora, his infant daughter, although they were surely with him in the city.

Soon Carl did return to the farm, where he made his living for many years. Although his interest in farming was diminished in later life when lightning struck and destroyed the barn, which was never rebuilt to its former stature, he stayed on the land, renting out pasture and doing some farm work for neighbors.

For a period of time in the 1940s, when the children were all grown and had families of their own, Carl and Nora went to California to live and work near their daughter, Cora. Their only son, Lewis, looked after the farm in their absence. Few details are known about this transition, which seems a little out of character for the Clarks. But they made the move just after the Second World War and only a year after the deaths of their daughter Fern and Nora's father, Charles Daily. It may be the middle-age couple was simply in need of change and an opportunity to recover from difficult times.

After all, 1944 had been a very difficult year for Carl and Nora. Their daughter Fern lost her infant son in April and Nora's father, Charles Daily, died in July. Fern's husband, Leon Moore, had written to her parents in July of 1943 when he and Fern were living in Whittier, California. "Fern is feeling pretty good," he wrote. "I think she's gotten along awfully good." But the state of getting better did not last. In December of 1944 Fern became ill and was treated at Dewitt Hospital in Waynesville, Missouri. Two days after Christmas, at age twenty-two, Fern died of complications from appendicitis.

The obituary noted that Fern had graduated from Richland High School in 1941, that she was married to Leon Moore, and that her baby, Robert Leon, had died at eight months of age. Fern was described as a "lovely and bright girl and her pleasant smile lingers with us yet." A few family members, including Ralph and Velma, who was then pregnant with her third child, were present during Fern's final moments of life.

On the front page of the *Lest We Forget* booklet provided by the funeral home, Nora wrote a few words about her daughter's passing.

Sister passed away quietly at 7 o'clock pm. Just as the sun went down, her life faded away. Her last words to mother were, rub my hand and arm, and to father she asked for a fire to warm her hands.

Later, photos were inserted between the pages of the booklet. One showed the young woman lying in her coffin outside the Clarks' home on a winter day. Nora added her own comments again, this time under the photo:

Taken where sister spent many hours playing. And my

dear little girl at rest. Gone but not forgotten by father or mother.

Fern's personal autograph book is inscribed by other students in study hall at Richland High in 1938 and filled with youthful whimsey, the kind of thing her friends knew she would appreciate. One wrote:

Dearest Fern
Ashes to ashes,Dust to Dust.
If it wasn't for kisses
Lips would rust.

Another writer made a reference to some secret past event:

Ain't it so? Or is it? Remember, Waynesville and the Model A roadster. Remember me always. B.J.

Years later, in the early 1970s, there came a day when Nora would indicate to Velma that she and Carl were having difficulty managing and they could no longer take care of themselves out on the farm. The details are not known, but life must have gotten very difficult for Nora to have even made the issue known. She kept much of her life private and seldom asked for assistance, but they were now isolated as never before. Carl could no longer drive. Their health had declined, and Carl's mental functions were diminishing. Caring for the farm was just no longer possible. Nora recognized the need to be nearer to town. At that point Ralph and Velma found a suitable apartment for the couple near their own home in Richland.

Carl and Nora's new home was a cozy one-bedroom apartment, and Nora was greatly relieved to be there. This was all the more remarkable since she had spent nearly her entire life on the farm. It was a great comfort to have, for the first time in her life, indoor plumbing.

Velma visited her parents frequently, as the apartment was only a short distance from her own home and she was pleased to care for them. Carl was still physically active and sometimes walked to Velma's house. On occasion he went with Ralph and the crew on a construction project as an observer.

The elderly couple would not live long in their apartment before Nora's demise. She had been suffering abdominal pain and was diagnosed with gallstones. She survived the gallbladder surgery and was sitting in a chair at the hospital awaiting discharge when she suddenly died. It is surmised that she died of a stroke, but an autopsy was not performed.

Nora was buried in the Hazelgreen Cemetery, which is also the burial site of her daughter, Fern; Carl's parents, Laverne and Belle; Carl's grandparents, Lewis and Mary; and later Carl himself.

Unable to live by himself any longer, Carl went to live for a time with his daughter, Cora, in Lindsay, California. During that time he continued to appear cheerful, although his mental and physical health had deteriorated. Feeling she was no longer able to care for him, Cora put Carl on a plane back to Missouri, where he would live with Ralph and Velma.

Carl's dementia continued to worsen. He could sometimes be found wandering in the abandoned chicken house, perhaps with fleeting memories of his early life on the farm. During Christmas dinner in 1972, when several guests were present, Carl looked very worn and tired, lacking his usual cheerful disposition. During the course of the dinner he was talking, but to no one in particular, creating words and sentences that made no sense to anyone. He was clearly lost to himself. After dinner he made a remark about the necessity of getting home, not realizing he was already there.

In addition to the problems associated with his dementia, he also became incontinent and was requiring a great deal of care. Finally Velma, who often suffered from back pain, reluctantly admitted that she could no longer provide all of his care. A place was found for her father in a nursing home in Lebanon, where he remained until his death on September 19, 1977.

MORE ABOUT NORA

Nora May Daily was born in Bethany, Missouri, on March 15, 1894. Her mother, Mary Ann Burris Daily, died in 1908 while Nora was a young teenager. Nora's father, Charles, later remarried. That relationship is clouded in mystery, but the impression was conveyed that it was not good; apparently, Charles and his second wife parted after a couple years.

For reasons unknown, and perhaps only because she resented another woman replacing her mother, Nora did not get along with her stepmother. Whatever the specific issues, Nora kept them to herself.

A single letter written by Mary Ann's father in May of 1892 sheds some light on himself and his daughter; in it, George Burris Jr. comes across as philosophical, mellow, caring, and lonely as he reports that he has just been to church where he has heard a good sermon. He wrote:

> *While it is rather discouraging to us on account of the rain and apparent bad for coughs, yet there is generally a bright side if we will view all things and on all sides... So I say there is always a bright side and as long as we have our health, we should be happy.*

He promised to write to Mary Ann often, although he thought he had little to say and no important news. Nevertheless, "it will be a letter from one who loves you." George also wrote that he was in fair health, "I think much better than last winter." But that state of affairs was soon to change; he died the following year at age sixty-eight and was buried in the Burris Cemetery in Harrison, Missouri.

Nora, who married Carl Clark on December 6, 1911, was in later life a large woman who moved slowly and cautiously. Even in old age she had fair skin, perhaps because she had always been careful to wear long sleeves and a large hat to protect herself from the sun when working outside with her flowers. She enjoyed quilting and was quite talented at crocheting, creating among other things a number of beautiful bedspreads. Her homemade bread was often enjoyed by visitors. She had once enjoyed cooking, but over the years lost interest in doing so, as she observed in a 1970 letter to her daughter, Cora, in California:

> Elize and Thelma here last Fr. from town. Got here as we got through eating dinner. So they ate scraps. Ha. No. It was good, better than they are used to. I made a rice pudding for dinner. They sure liked it. I had baked L. bread and vegetables enough for them and sausage. Alice fixed my hair last week. I was over there. My your dinner sounded good... Pop says that's lots of work, and it is, but I always liked to cook. Am almost fizzled now. I took Alice a big chocolate pie. She claims she can't make them. She was glad to get it.

Nora appreciated her family, but she did not enjoy or tolerate the rowdiness of children and expected young visitors to maintain some decorum. In another letter to Cora, she noted that some of the grandchildren who had visited Velma recently had been unruly. Velma had said, she wrote, that in the confusion she burned two pie crusts. Nora concluded that such children should be made to behave, and suggested that were she in Velma's place, Nora would make such corrections occur.

Most of Nora's social contacts were old friends she had known since childhood, as well as longtime neighbors, her own children, and some of her surviving siblings.

Two of her sisters, Dot and Pearl, as well as her brother George, all lived in Marshfield, Missouri, and occasional visits were made.

As an older woman Nora was often viewed by her grandchildren as rather stern, perhaps aloof, not given to overt affection, reserved in her praise, and not nearly as approachable as her fun-loving spouse. Given that impression, it is helpful to imagine her as a young woman, a teenager around fourteen years of age, perhaps in love, and soon to marry and enter the adult world. That relatively happy time is reflected in a small homemade book containing notes from her classmates that was presented to her in 1909 at the Laquey School by her friend Hattie Nichols. Nora was already seeing Carl Clark, as one friend noted:

> *Dear Nora*
> *Live on Love,*
> *Drink on wind.*
> *When you get Carl*
> *The Way You squeeze him*
> *Will be a sin.*

Another person wrote:

> *Hogs love pumpkins,*

Cows love squash.
Carl loves you,
He does, by gosh.

And another friend wrote:

Dear Miss Clark,
When you and C gets married and C gets cross
Pick up the broom and say
I'm the boss.

The entries in this keepsake are reminders that Nora was once young, and although she was troubled by her mother's death and unhappy with her new stepmother, she had friends, was hopeful, and looked forward to a new life. One thing is certain, the teenager was already involved with Carl Clark and had marriage on her mind. She valued the small book enough to keep it her entire life.

CHARLES M. DAILY

NORA'S FATHER WAS also a farmer. According to Donald Daily, son of Nora's brother George Daily, "Charles was wiry, about five foot eight inches. He had an eighth grade education, and he chewed tobacco."

Charles's parents were William and Sarah A. Daily, and he was born in Harrison, Missouri. William Daily listed Tennessee as his birthplace, and Sarah was born in Virginia.

In the last years of his life Charles lived with his son George, who had built a special addition to his own home for Charles. At age eighty-five, the elder Daily died of cancer after declining to see a doctor long after his illness became known. He was buried alongside his wife, Mary Ann Burris, in the Iduma Cemetery in Laquey, Missouri.

THE STORY OF INDIAN JOE

IN MAY OF 1964 Dot McKay Daily, Nora's sister, wrote a letter to Nora in which she enclosed a newspaper article about John Ewing, who was also known as Indian Joe. Dot wrote:

> *Indian John Ewing was so called because he was stolen by the Indians. He was the father of our grandmother, Lydia Ewing Burris.*

So begins the true story of one of Velma's ancestors, an interesting story that, for some reason, was never shared with the children. That was surely one story that would have excited the kids. Sure, they saw plenty of "cowboy and Indian" shows on TV, but to have their very own relative the subject of a kidnapping who went on to live with his captors would have been something worth knowing. Perhaps Nora did not herself know the story until later in life, and perhaps it was still later for Velma. Or it may be that they simply did not think it useful to talk of such things. The Clark family was not one that talked much about the past.

There are a number of versions of the story of John's kidnapping, and while some of the details vary (and may even have been enhanced throughout the years), the inciting incident is known as the Clendenin Massacre.[6]

John Ewing was born in Virginia in 1747. Around 1764, when he was still a youth, he and his sister Nancy were kidnapped by Shawnee warriors near Lewisburg, West Virginia. At the time of the massacre, Nancy managed to escape, but her husband and child were killed. John was kidnapped and then adopted by the warrior who kidnapped him. He lived with the tribe for around three years, then was released as part of a treaty between the British and the Shawnee.

And now the details, or at least one version of them: As a young man, John worked on his father's farm. He loved to read, and even though his family could not afford the luxury of books, the local Presbyterian minister allowed him to use his library. The lad was said to have a remarkable memory, and even in old age he was able to quote long passages from *Paradise Lost*.

John was visiting his sister, Nancy, and her husband, Archibald Clendenin, who had acquired a large acreage. On that fateful day, John was in the field, hoeing corn beside two slaves. Around noon the workers heard shots coming from the house and they immediately went to investigate. Upon approaching the house, they saw several Native Americans, which was not in itself alarming, as friendly Natives sometimes visited the settlements. This time, though, something was terribly wrong.

Nancy had been tied to a horse. Her husband lay dead and scalped nearby. The Natives were holding her infant son. In the confusion, a horse fell and Nancy was able to escape. She ran, hiding in the forest. The Natives quickly responded by killing the infant they held in their arms. After evading a black bear, Nancy made her way back to the cabin, which had been burned to the ground. Her husband's body, his dog standing watch at his side, remained on the ground where he had been killed. After burying his body she sought protection from nearby soldiers.

Meanwhile, John had been taken captive. After a long journey to his captor's home, he was made to run the gauntlet and was then beaten by the young males of the tribe. After a time, though, he became the adopted son of the warrior who took him prisoner. He would later describe the warrior as a highly intelligent, upright, and honorable man.

John learned the Shawnee language, and when a Bible was brought back from a raid, the tribal chief asked him to translate some of the passages and to explain their meanings. After John read from Genesis about the creation, the chief asked whether the first man was white or Indian. John responded that it must have been a white man, which the Chief found absurd. "I pity your ignorance," the chief said, "but you ought at least to have sense enough to know that the Great Spirit never made the poor, ignorant, cowardly white man before he did the red man." But the Chief asked him to continue. When John came to the story of Noah and the great flood, the only Shawnee word he could come up with for ark was canoe. Now the chief was clearly skeptical. "Now, you know that is a lie; there never was a tree on the Scioto Bottoms big enough to make such a canoe as that."[7]

During John Ewing's time with the Shawnee, the village was devastated by smallpox. John was stricken, but he survived. After nearly three years of hunting and farming in captivity, he was released. He made his way to a settlement, where he was furnished with clothing, and then reunited with his mother and sister, who were glad and astonished to see him alive.

It would have been wonderful if John Ewing, educated as he was, had written an account of his time with the Shawnee. He did not do so, leaving us to speculate about the details. Despite the unquestionable terror of being kidnapped and seeing his brother-in-law killed, he seems to have survived the ordeal quite well. It is also remarkable that he was favored by the chief and became his interpreter, and that he spent his time with his captors hunting and farming, which he would likely have been doing on his own.

In a fictional version of the tale we would likely hear how Ewing was conflicted in his feelings in regard to his captors, and perhaps that he had difficulty reentering white society. All we do know is that the man who came to be known as Indian Joe later married a woman named Ann Smith, with whom he raised a large family and lived a quiet life as a farmer. He died in 1824 and was buried near Vinton, Ohio.

One of John's daughters, Lydia Ewing, was born in 1790. She married George Burris, who was born in Virginia in the same year. Together they had ten children and were said to have had a very good marriage. Lydia died in 1872 in Bethany, Missouri, a few months after her husband.

George Burris was a farmer and served in the War of 1812. In 1832 he was elected to the Ohio Legislature and the next year was appointed judge to the courts. When he was sixty-seven years of age, he and Lydia moved by covered wagon from Ohio, where he had lived for most of his life, to Bethany Township, Missouri, where his sons had earlier settled.

One of George and Lydia's sons, George Burris Jr., fathered eight children. His daughter Mary Ann later married Charles Martin Daily and became the mother of eight children, including Nora May Clark.

John Ewing, also known as Indian Joe, who was kidnapped by the Shawnee and lived in captivity for a number of years, was therefore the grandfather, several times removed, of Velma Clark Posten.

THE POSTENS
PHOEBE AND THE BOSTWICKS

RALPH POSTEN'S MOTHER, Phoebe, was born February 14, 1879, in Butler County, Kansas. Previous to Phoebe's birth, her parents and five siblings had moved to Kansas from Hamden, a small village in the Catskill Mountains in New York State.

Phoebe's father, Oscar Kellogg Bostwick, was born in New York State in 1826 and died in 1908. Her mother, Matilda Cruickshank Bostwick, was born in 1839 in Troy, New York, to John C. Cruikshank and Charlotte Cotheal Ayres, and died in 1911. Matilda was buried in Guthrie, Oklahoma, where she had gone to live with one of her children.

In 1860, when Phoebe's father was thirty-four years of age and not yet married, he lived with his siblings; his parents, Marcus L. and Deborah Bostwick; and his seventy-eight-year-old widowed grandmother, Freelove Frisbee Bostwick.

Freelove's late husband, Jabez Bostwick, was born in Stratford, Connecticut, in 1778 and died in 1856 in Hamden, New York, where he operated a store and owned a farm. He also served as a schools inspector, was elected Justice of the Peace, and was the first judge of the Delaware County Courts.

THE OIL MAN: JABEZ ABEL BOSTWICK

THERE HAS BEEN no relative of the Posten family more wealthy than Jabez Abel Bostwick, the nephew of Phoebe Posten's great-grandfather. One could write his story simply as a poor farm boy who went to the big city and through hard work and keen intelligence made a fortune, but a critical writer might insist that Jabez Abel Bostwick was a part of a small group that collaborated to make decisions, often in secret, that would monopolize the oil business and push competitors to the side, making fortunes for themselves, often at the expense of others. It is true that Jabez was a poor farm boy who attained a seat of power through his involvement in an elite group that created Standard Oil.

It is best simply to tell the man's story and let others make whatever judgments they think necessary.

Abel Bostwick was brother to Jabez Bostwick, Phoebe Posten's great-grandfather. Abel had a family of his own, and named one of his sons Jabez Abel Bostwick. It was that son who was to take an entirely different path than that of his farming family.

Jabez Abel was born in Delaware County, New York, then moved with his family to Ohio. His father was a farmer of modest means. Jabez Abel did not like farm life and sought a different way to make a living. As a youth he found work as a clerk in a bank. Later he entered the hardware business in Cleveland. In the 1850s he became a cotton dealer in Cincinnati, as well as a grain buyer for another firm. He then went into the cotton brokerage business, moving to New York City in 1864, where he was a cotton dealer in association with J.B. Tilford. The firm was named Bostwick and Tilford; by 1872, the firm was the largest oil buyer in New York.

Bostwick, who clearly had a sharp eye for business trends, studied the prospects for petroleum and imagined soaring demand and profitable investments. He began dealing in oil, investing in wells in Franklin, Pennsylvania. When John D. Rockefeller formed the Standard Oil Company in 1872, Jabez joined him and aided in its creation after dissolving Bostwick and Tilford. Jabez would later become secretary/treasurer of the Standard Oil Trust.

It was not by accident that Jabez Bostwick became associated with John D. Rockefeller; Jabez was handpicked because of what he brought to the table. Rockefeller is reported to have said, "I tried to attract only the able men and I have always had little as possible to do with dull business men."[8] While that was true, it did not hurt that Bostwick brought with him exactly the resources Rockefeller needed at the time to consolidate Standard Oil.

One of Bostwick's associates said that he was "strict almost to sternest in his dealing, preferring justice to sentiment."[9] Such a characterization would no doubt fit well with Rockefeller's own personality. A shrewd businessman himself, Bostwick had already guessed the future of oil and started investing in it. As one writer observed, "Rockefeller had literally raided the oil business and confiscated all its brains."[10] Bostwick fit the description and was among the chosen ones Rockefeller needed to make Standard Oil the prosperous enterprise it was to become.

There were other reasons Rockefeller felt comfortable with Jabez Bostwick. Both were born in New York and had been moved with their families to Ohio, where each had started his own business. Both had eventually moved back to New York. They shared the experience of having been born into a poor family. Rockefeller was one of six children; his father, often absent, was a lumberman and traveling salesman, his mother a fervent Baptist. Bostwick, who was nine years older than Rockefeller, came from a family of five and was the son of farmers and devoted Baptists. Rockefeller began his career as a bookkeeper; Bostwick started out as a bank clerk.

Both men had a sharp eye for business, to which they were wholeheartedly devoted. Despite huge financial success and busy lives, both were vigilant about attending church regularly. Rockefeller even sometimes took notes during sermons and presented them to his wife when she was unable to attend. Both men spent long days at the office and had little time for outside activities and friends, but on Wednesday nights you could be certain that each man would be present at prayer service at his own church. Rockefeller and Bostwick shared a dedication to hard work and a reliance on faith, regardless of their critics and other social pressures. Neither man was aware of any contradiction between his religion and the enterprise in which he was engaged.

Rockefeller's fortune far exceeded Bostwick's, but both were generous with charitable contributions. Rockefeller helped create a new era of philanthropy in response to public disdain of the Standard Trust. The Baptists were early recipients of both men's giving, and in addition to what they provided to their individual churches, Rockefeller funded a small Baptist school that eventually grew to be the acclaimed University of Chicago. Bostwick was a benefactor to Wake Forest College in North Carolina, where a residence hall bears his name.

For many years Bostwick was the primary oil buyer for Standard Oil. He retired in 1885 and was elected president of the New York and New England Railroad Company. He also had a seat on the New York Stock Exchange.

It was after his retirement from Standard Oil that accusations of the company's ruthless, predatory, and monopolistic tactics were made in full force. Investigative journalists like Ida Tarbell and Henry Lloyd published revelations of the companies' actions and invoked the public's scorn.[11,12] It was no secret that Rockefeller himself planned to monopolize the oil business, according to biographer John T. Flynn.[13] The subject of the Standard Oil Trust became hotly debated, arousing public wrath and inciting legislative action.

In 1879 a grand jury in Pennsylvania indicted Rockefeller, Bostwick, and several others for criminal conspiracy. The accused used a number of legal tactics to avoid answering questions that might have led to their convictions, including invoking the right not to incriminate themselves. The New York Senate started its own investigation in 1888, and soon afterward the House of Representatives followed with its own inquiry, eventually calling Rockefeller and Bostwick to the witness stand, among others.

In 1890, Congress passed the Sherman Antitrust Act, which allowed the government to dissolve trusts. In 1882, the

Ohio Supreme Court declared the Standard Oil Trust an illegal monopoly and ordered it dissolved.

Matthew Josephson described the group of men, the power brokers of the age, as "Robber Barons"; in his estimation they had many of the same traits as feudal barons of yore. Their conduct was not constrained by the common moral codes of the day. Often lawless, they made decisions and took actions that were based on their own rules of business. In effect, they created their own rules. Josephson nevertheless admits that through their inventive planning, organizing, and manipulation of resources and workers, they got together unorganized and wasteful portions of the economy and created a centralized, efficient system of production. Despite all criticism, these men can be said to have been the midwives of the industrial age, and yet they were guilty of seeking private gain that resulted in "much disaster, outrage, and misery."[14]

Others, including John T. Flynn in his sympathetic biography, took a different view, stating that the Rockefeller fortune was "the most honestly acquired" of all the great fortunes of the day.[15]

Rockefeller's connection to Jabez Abel Bostwick makes him relevant to this family history despite the absence of actual family ties, because much of the criticism of Rockefeller was also directed at his close associates. Even so, Rockefeller had no problem reconciling his religion with his business tactics; on the contrary, he often spoke of business in religious terms, declaring that Standard Oil had been "Godlike," acting in the role of a missionary for the world.[16] It is likely that the equally devout Bostwick was also at ease with the union of Christianity and capitalism.

TRAGIC DEATH

AT THE TIME of Jabez Abel Bostwick's untimely and tragic death in 1892, the New York papers, including the *New York Times*, the *New York Star* and the *New York Tribune*, gave detailed accounts of his life and death.

Described as a self-made man, Bostwick was said to have been an inventive businessman who paid close attention to detail and was upright and honest in his dealings. He abstained from alcohol and tobacco. As a faithful member of the Fifth Avenue Baptist Church, he never missed a Sunday service and was a great financial benefactor to the church and other charitable causes. He believed education helped make people more self-reliant and supported education for women; one of his daughters learned dressmaking and another became a medical doctor.

Dr. Armitage, a longtime friend and a pastor of the Fifth Avenue Baptist Church, officiated at Bostwick's funeral and emphasized "his staunch, unchangeable character as a friend and his simple lovable disposition under all circumstances."[17]

It was on the night of August 16, 1892, that the retired businessman's life came to a sudden and unexpected end. He and his wife were staying at their summer home in Mamaroneck on Long Island Sound. The couple had entertained guests that evening and then gone to bed. Shortly after they retired, they were roused from their sleep and notified that smoke had been detected and that fire had broken out in Bostwick's stables and those of his neighbor, James Constable. There was a mad dash to save horses and property. In the midst of the chaos, Bostwick, who was trying to help save the carriages, suffered an injury and was carried into his house and placed on the sofa. The eight horses and twelve carriages were rescued, but Bostwick was in pain and had suffered a serious injury. A doctor was called but could do little, and the injured man reported pain in his back. Shortly before his death he said, "How will this end? How will this end?"[18] He died shortly thereafter.

The fire was brought under control after it destroyed both of Bostwick's stables and the neighbor's carriage house, carriages, and horses. The charred bodies of two of Mr. Constable's servants were discovered later; they had recently arrived from Ireland and were asleep in the room above the carriage house. The fire was determined to be accidental, as there was hay in both stables that could have easily caught fire from even a small spark.

There was a debate as to whether the millionaire died of heart failure, for which he had been treated, or from injuries received in his efforts to rescue a carriage from the blaze. The cause of death was ultimately determined to be an injury to a blood vessel in the spinal cord.

The *New York Times* reported that a large number of friends from the city took a train from Grand Central Station to the station at Mamaroneck, where they were met by carriages and conveyed to the family's summer home for the funeral. Among the mourners were Bostwick's colleagues at Standard Oil, including William Rockefeller, H.M. Flagler, J.D. Archibald, and H.H. Rogers. Noticeably absent was John D. Rockefeller. Bostwick's brother, Abel Bostwick, traveled from Ohio to attend the services.[19] Bostwick's two daughters, who were in Europe at the time of his death, missed the funeral but immediately boarded a ship bound for the United States.

At the time of his death, Bostwick's estate was estimated at around ten million dollars. In 1927, upon the death of his widow, it was valued at over twenty-nine million dollars, including twenty million dollars' worth of Standard Oil stock. The Bostwick mansion, described as a "French Empire beauty," was located on Fifth Avenue at the corner of 61st Street, ten blocks north of Central Park. The structure was later torn down and a condo tower was built in its place.[20]

MORE ABOUT PHOEBE

IT IS NOT known whether Phoebe Bostwick Posten, who was still a young girl at the time of Jabez Abel Bostwick's death, knew the history of her wealthy relative. It is also a mystery whether other members of the family in Hamden, in the Ozarks, or elsewhere maintained any contact with their prosperous kin, a true tycoon who perhaps deserved the dubious moniker of "robber baron." There is no evidence that any of his wealth found its way into their far more modest coffers.

In a remarkable coincidence, another link in the Posten-Clark story was involved in the birth of the oil industry, but under much different circumstances. Benjamin Avery Posten's part was to work in the early days of the oil fields in Pennsylvania, to labor in the mud, breathe air toxic with oil fumes, walk in oily slime, and sleep in a crowded shack, all in anticipation of receiving perhaps a dollar a day for his efforts. That story is still to come.

While Jabez A. Bostwick was achieving his great success, life went on as usual for the extended family. By 1870, his cousin Oscar Bostwick had married Matilda Cruikshank, some sixteen years his junior, fathered three children, and was living in Sonoma, California. Oscar and Matilda moved next to Butler County, Kansas, where Phoebe was born. Later the family would move to Pulaski County, Missouri, where Phoebe would meet Mart Posten. She was around fifteen years of age when they were married on July 7, 1894. Around that time, Phoebe's brother, Oscar Kellogg Bostwick Jr., married Bessie May, another offspring of Benjamin Avery Posten.

Phoebe is remembered with special reverence by her grand-children and was highly respected and loved by her own children. Hardworking, devoted, loyal, and humble, with a gentle nature and always looking after the welfare of others, Phoebe was entirely the dutiful wife, waiting tirelessly to attend to her husband's every need. She lived her life in what would now be considered primitive conditions and gave birth to twelve children, three of whom died in infancy, and at least as was observed in their old age, got little support from Mart. Phoebe did not talk much about the past, but she did tell of coming to Missouri in a covered wagon and of later riding her horse to the dentist, having all her teeth pulled, and returning home. A memorable ride, no doubt.

On Christmas Day 1894, just fifteen years old and five months married, Phoebe wrote a letter to a sibling expressing her desire to see them and sounding a little homesick.

> I wish you could have been here to spend Christmas with me. I would like to see your girl too. Well I think her name is real pretty. They are some working on the church house today. Was there snow on the ground there today. There was not any here. Mother and pop and Artie spent their Christmas with Aunt S... Artie is going to start to Springfield tomorrow to stay with Sadie awhile... We are

spending our first Christmas night by ourselves. Your sister, Phoebe Posten.

Phoebe cooked, cleaned, did the laundry, managed the garden, took care of the chickens, and did everything else that needed to be done to manage the family and care for her husband. In the summer in later years, she and Velma Posten canned produce from the garden and fruit from the orchard and stored it in a dirt cellar under the house, safe from the freezing winters.

There was a spring a short distance from the house, and before the introduction of electricity to the house, Phoebe would sometimes send her grandson Eddie Posten, a frequent visitor, to submerge a jug of milk in its cool water. When weather permitted and necessity demanded, she built a large open fire outside, placed on it a large iron kettle, and made soap by combining lye, water, and lard. The soap was used for all her household and personal cleaning needs. She would heat water in the same pot when it was time to do the family laundry, and that with the help of only a scrub board. She never owned a power washing machine of any kind.

In old age, following Mart's death in 1953, Phoebe moved from the home place and began a time of living with her children. One would take her for a time, then move her on to the next one. The family considered this method a way of sharing the responsibilities of caretaking, but it was a process that was likely confusing to the elderly woman, no matter the good intentions of her children. Even so, the alternative would have been to place her in a nursing home, and there was a family tradition of elders living with their children in old age. Oscar, Phoebe's father, had been raised in a household that included his grandmother, Freelove Bostwick. And Matilda, Phoebe's own mother, spent her last days living with one of her offspring.

When it was Ralph and Velma's time to do the caretaking, they were living in the house Velma's grandfather, Luverne Clark, built many years earlier. Phoebe had her own room, which was filled with a portion of her own modest furnishings. She was expected to share meals with the family, but she often set the table in her own room, as though anticipating a guest for dinner or perhaps getting dinner ready for Mart as she had done for so many years. At times she could be heard to call out for Mart, urging him to put away the horses and come in for dinner.

Death came on August 1, 1962, at the age of eighty-three after years of declining health. Phoebe had long suffered from a marked curvature of the back. In old photos she appears partially bent over. Without question she suffered from other health issues, some related to having borne so many children, but Phoebe was not one to complain and much of her suffering was in silence. If she was asked how she was doing, her familiar reply was "fair to middlin'." In her last year she often sat quietly, many times by herself. To an observer she seemed sad, maybe depressed, or perhaps just weary of life. Her death certificate reported her cause of death was arteriosclerosis. Phoebe was buried beside Mart in the Fairview Cemetery.

BOSTWICKS COME TO AMERICA

In 1901 Henry Anton Bostwick wrote a considerably detailed book about the history of the Bostwick family in which he confirmed that Phoebe's father, Oscar, and her grandfather, Marcus Lucius, were direct descendants of an original settler in America, Arthur Bostwick.[21]

Arthur Bostwick was born in 1603 in Cheshire County, England, and took the long voyage to America around 1639, less than twenty years after the Pilgrims landed at Plymouth Rock.

The Puritans had been in much distress in Europe, facing intense persecution from the church, and it is likely that the hostile environment had something to do with Arthur's search for a place of freedom. Many thousands had left Europe for just that reason.

Arthur Bostwick is listed as one of the first seventeen settlers in Stratford, Connecticut. He was around thirty-six years of age upon arrival in America. His marital status upon arrival is unclear; some accounts suggest he was unmarried, and perhaps a widower. Another account indicates otherwise. In any case, he had a son by the name of John.

If Arthur was married upon his arrival in America, his wife may have soon died, for he was known to later marry a widow by the name of Ellen Johnson. In later life, in 1674, he and Ellen signed a legal document dividing their property in order to leave their portions to their children by previous marriages. Arthur gave most of what he owned to his son, but he made several stipulations to ensure that his son would take care of him in his old age. By contract his son agreed to "maintain his father with whatever he shall need for comfort" and "to find him wines and spirituous liquors and a horse when he shall wish to ride forth," among other provisions.[22]

When Arthur arrived at his new home, which was later named Stratford, Connecticut, there were many Native Americans in the area. This had been, after all, their home before Europeans started moving in. There were numerous disputes over land ownership, some of which were not resolved until many years later. The Stratford group had been organized in 1639 at Wethersfield and Hartford, Connecticut, and probably consisted of seventeen families. Being among the first settlers had its advantages, as records show that over time Arthur acquired considerable land holdings.

The group, composed mostly of farmers, had come to America primarily to escape religious oppression, yet the settlement had its own issues with religious bigotry. Perhaps the worst of their actions was the persecution and execution of women accused of witchcraft. During this period witch hysteria had taken hold in a number of places throughout the world.

AN HISTORIC HOME

PHOEBE'S GREAT-GRANDMOTHER FREELOVE Frisbee, who was later to marry Jabez Bostwick, grew up in what was to become an historic home. The details of this home and the family who lived in it are provided in information released by Delaware County Historical Association in New York.[23]

The Frisbee family were early settlers in Delaware County and were descendants of Congregationalist Puritans whose arrival in America dated back to the seventeenth century. Freelove's grandfather, Phillip Frisbee, had been a major in the Revolutionary War, serving as a captain in the Seventeenth Regiment of the New York State Militia. After the war he was elected to the New York State Assembly.

Freelove's father, Gideon, also served in the Revolutionary War. Gideon married Huldah Kidder, by whom he fathered Freelove and her five siblings. After the death of Huldah in July of 1804, Gideon married a neighbor's young daughter, who was also named Freelove, and with her added six more children to his brood.

Gideon had settled in Delaware County and come to be the owner of a large estate that may have been part of his reward for serving in the war. He first built a sawmill and a log house, the latter of which was eventually used as a tavern for travelers. Around 1797 he built a fine house, "rather prominent in style, mirroring Gideon's position in the local community."[24] He continued to farm while serving as one of the judges on the Court of Common Pleas and as county treasurer.

The house was not only the home for all his children, but it also served as the site of the court until a courthouse was constructed. In addition, the house was the location for many public functions. The claim has been made that the Frisbee House is "The birthplace of Delaware County."[25]

Although the Frisbee house remained in the family for many years, due to financial hardship it was eventually sold to individuals outside the family. It became part of the Delaware County Historical Association in the 1960s and was placed on the National Register of Historic Places in 1975.

MARTIN KING POSTEN

MART, AS HE was known, was seventy-nine years old when he died on September 11, 1953. Witnesses of his life who are living today remember him as an old man and can only guess at what he might have done and been like at a younger age. In those later years, Mart, clad in his familiar overalls, could often be found sitting on the front porch smoking his pipe. Sometimes he would sit there with his single-barrel twelve-gauge shotgun in hand, hoping to shoot any unlucky rabbits that wandered too close to the house. Other reasons for maintaining his perch included overseeing a hired hand chop his firewood, or listening as youth from the church sang gospel songs for him. Whatever the reasons, the front porch was his favorite place to be outdoors.

Inside the house his favorite chair was a rocking chair situated on one side of the wood stove, which, as the only source of heat in the house, had a prominent place in the living room. To his right stood a single table, upon which he kept an ashtray, a resting place for his pipe and tobacco, and his used chewing gum. On the wall just above his chair was the family clock, the source of a monotonous ticking remembered by the grandchildren who endured it during long afternoon visits. On one wall was a painting of Jesus holding a lamb. A large and impressive frame housed a photo of Lina Lee, one of the children who died in infancy and the lastborn of the twelve.

The living room, which they called the "front room," also housed Mart and Phoebe's bed and served as their bedroom. This was a comfort measure. The unpainted clapboard house had no insulation and its single bedroom was frigid in winter. Much too cold for the elderly couple, though it was used for overnight visitors. In cold weather, Phoebe provided an extra feather comforter for visitors.

Mart had been a lifelong farmer, though he was not very successful in that occupation. The farm had been lost during the Depression and then saved due to the generosity of a daughter, Nettie Wakefield, who paid the taxes and took over as owner of the property, providing her parents free lodging for as long as they remained in the house.

In his later years, Mart had a series of strokes, the last of which took his life. Before the final stroke he managed well enough, taking walks with his cane for assistance, and he received ongoing wait services from Phoebe, which she performed without complaint even though she too had struggles and was often not feeling well.

At times Mart did show some signs that he was aware of his dependence on his wife. In one such instance Phoebe was feeling ill and still rushing around to do all of her chores while Mart stood idle and watched her walk down the path to the chicken house. With a worried look the elderly man turned to Eddie and Don, grandsons who were visiting at the time. "Watch Grandma," he said. "We might lose her." The young boys did not understand what he was saying. To them, their grandfather had just indicated their grandmother might be leaving, going away, taking a trip, which made no sense at all. It did not occur to them at that young age that Mart might be considering what was really important and feeling anxious about what life would be like without the support of his faithful spouse.

All of the Posten children were frequent visitors, and always welcome. They were often given Wrigley's chewing gum as a special treat; a large supply was always kept inside a chest of drawers next to the bed.

The grandfather could be quite tyrannical at times, an imposing figure. In one instance he became displeased with something Carl had done or not done; perhaps he'd failed to obey a command. The elderly man raised his cane high in the air as if to strike the child. "God could strike you down right now," he declared, before lowering his cane.

Although not gifted with a good singing voice, he was fond of sharing short ditties and did so often. One of his favorites was an old folk song.

The Old Gray Mare
Oh the old gray mare, she ain't what she used to be.
Ain't what she used to be. Ain't what she used to be.
The old gray mare, she ain't what she used to be.
Many long years ago.
Another of Mart's favorites:
Go tell Aunt Rhody, old grey goose is dead.
One she's been saving, saving for a bed.
Go tell Aunt Rhody, old gray goose is dead.
One she's been saving for a bed.
Go tell Aunt Rhody. Go tell Aunt Rhody.
Go tell Aunt Rhody. Old grey goose is dead.

Mart was well regarded in the Hazelgreen community, and was one of the original members of the Independence Baptist Church, which was organized in 1921. The only two books in the house were the Bible, a cornerstone of his religious faith, and *Uncle Tom's Cabin,* which was perhaps a link to his own father's stand on slavery and participation in the Civil War.

Martin King Posten was regarded as a man of great faith, but even so, one of the tales told of him is difficult to accept at face value. One longtime church member and a friend to Mart emphasized the powerful faith of the man by telling the story of Mart driving his wagon and team of horses to town one day. The weather turned bad and there was a great thunderstorm, hard rain; a major obstacle to travel. Apparently the man did not like to get wet or have his trip delayed; he confronted the storm and commanded the rain to stop, which it did without delay.

Whatever may have been Mart's faith and character in those days, it is highly unlikely that control of the weather was one of his attributes. The cessation of a rainstorm can easily be attributed to natural fluctuations in the weather, but the church member was convinced that it was Mart's faith that did the trick. And that points to the true significance of the story: that a natural occurrence would be earnestly and repeatedly reported by an intelligent, respected member of the community, and probably by others as well, as an act of faith, indicated the high regard in which Mart was held. He may not have had such great clout with the weather, but there was something about the man—his character, his presence, the way he spoke—something that impressed people and led them to consider that he just might be well enough aligned with cosmic forces to halt a rainstorm if he so willed it. It is as one old-timer commented: "When he spoke, he spoke with authority."

Once when Eddie and Don were spending the night with their grandparents, a bad storm was being predicted, dire warnings of rain and damaging wind. Night approached and the storm grew closer. This time Mart made no such command upon the storm. Rather, he instructed the children to exit the bedroom, where they normally slept on their visits, and sleep instead on the couch in the living room. "If we go, we'll all go together," he said; words that were perhaps intended to comfort but instead left the children feeling anxious.

For many years there was a huge family reunion at Mart and Phoebe's home in honor of his birthday on August 12. This occasion brought together all of the couple's children who lived within driving distance. In some years, relatives from California and Oklahoma also arrived for the event. There were cousins by the score, and also neighbors and friends from the church. Since the reunion was held in August, usually the hottest and most humid month in Missouri, the food was placed outside in the shade on two long tables. This was a necessary arrangement in any case as the kitchen was far too small to accommodate the crowd. The outside venue also welcomed scores of flies, bees, and other creatures of the air who knew a feast when they saw it. The visiting children played, the women stayed busy with last-minute food preparation, and the men smoked and spoke of guns, work, cars, and sometimes religion. The birthday celebration did not fail to be a grand event that was looked forward to and enjoyed by its participants.

The reunion continued for many years after Mart's death, eventually moving to Bennett Spring State Park, and finally, as the participants grew older and fewer and fewer relatives came at all, to air-conditioned settings in Richland and Hazelgreen. The character of the event changed over the years as well. What had once been a time to celebrate now invoked a sense of obligation. It was as if all the energy had departed from the occasion. The day came when few people showed up and no one wanted to be the organizer, and the reunion faded into memory.

In the days following Mart's last stroke, he lay in his own bed, dying. Numerous family members gathered to say their goodbyes and observe his passing. The small house was crowded with people coming and going, standing around, quietly chatting, trying to stay out of the way of everyone else. At times Mart would become conscious and call for a member of the family by name, who would come to his bedside for a final farewell.

With Mart's death, there were but two surviving children of Benjamin Avery and Mary Ellen Posten. Artie Belle, who had been married to William Gan, died in 1965. Her sister, Alice Blanche, who had been part of a set of triplets, married Lee Hatfield, and died in 1964.

As Mart requested, a stalagmite that he had long ago taken from a local cave and that stood prominently for years under the front porch was used to mark his grave. Later, a more traditional monument was added. The bill for the funeral from Hedges Funeral Home came to $521.84.

Any attempt to overly romanticize life on the farm for Phoebe and Mart takes issue with reality. In many respects, theirs was a hard life that only grew more problematic as they aged. Phoebe had borne twelve children. The first child, Clarence, was born in 1895 and died six months later. The last two, Leland in 1922 and Linda Lee in 1924, both died within two years of their birth.

The farm was never the best of land, and it was lost during the Depression. The house was heated with wood, which was easily obtainable from the forests nearby provided one was able to do the work. For most of their lives they had no phone. They grew some of their food early on, but not much in later life. They did not drive and never owned an automobile; they were totally dependent on their children for transportation. There were few expenses, but little income. In a day when there was little social safety net, the elderly depended upon the compassion, or guilt, of their children for care in their old age. The couple died before the arrival of Medicare and never had health insurance of any kind. A doctor was seen only in the event of a serious health crisis, and hospitals were avoided. No dental care. No dentist. In late life they did receive a small pension, which came about as a result of the Social Security Act of 1935. In sum, Mart and Phoebe Posten lived in rural poverty, and especially as they aged, they depended heavily upon the benevolence of their children.

If they were prosperous, and there is an argument that they were, it was in the sense of community. Despite their relative isolation from the outside world, Mart and Phoebe's adherence to certain traditions, cultural values, and their brand of religion, plus the collective benefits of a strong faith community, a large extended family, and longstanding neighbors who lived in close proximity, enabled them to enjoy a social life and supportive network the likes of which money cannot buy.

Life on the farm in the Ozarks was often difficult and times were changing. It is no accident that all three of the couple's sons—Lewis, Ralph, and Clyde—had no enthusiasm for farm life. As soon as they were able and alternatives were available, they all sought their livelihoods elsewhere.

OZARK PIONEERS: MARY ELLEN DEAN AND BENJAMIN AVERY POSTEN

BENJAMIN AVERY AND Mary Ellen would in time make their way to Missouri and there in the Ozarks establish a base for a large family for generations to come. But they started out in Pennsylvania and had to survive the Civil War before they could make the Ozarks their home.

PENNSYLVANIA DUTCH

One of the things known about the Ralph Posten family was that Benjamin Avery Posten was Pennsylvania Dutch. That much was an oral tradition in the family, but the term was never really understood or explained. There was often an assumption that the family was related to the Dutch, but this was a common misunderstanding.

The Pennsylvania Dutch did not come from Holland. They had nothing to do with the city of Amsterdam and they were not Dutch. They were, at least in a broad, general sense, German. As a group they came to America in large numbers between 1683 and the 1800s. They were an ethnic group, a German-speaking people from a number of countries: western and southern Germany, but also from the eastern regions of France, Switzerland, Austria, Belgium, and even Holland.[26]

Many came from the Palatinate state of Germany on the German Rhine. This area was settled by Celtic and Germanic people and incorporated by the Roman Empire in the first century. The Palatinate had a long history as a center of contention among a number of nations, including Bavaria, Spain, and France.

There are a number of factors that might have added to the confusion about the term. A dialect of German was spoken, and was referred to as "Deutsch," which is the German word for Dutch. It is easy to see how outsiders might have been confused by the word itself. Also, the Pennsylvania Dutch sailed to America out of ports in the Netherlands, which may have led others to conclude they originated from Holland.[27]

The Pennsylvania Dutch came to America to escape economic woes and religious persecution. Included in the group were Morovians, Anabaptists, Amish, and members of the Church of the Brethren, but the majority were Lutheran or Reformed. All were beckoned by William Tell's promises of religious tolerance.

This was a very conservative group, mostly farmers, who centered their lives on family, religion, and rural life. The center of their lives was the place where they lived, not the greater United States. As a group they did not trust strangers, and the majority did not support Abraham Lincoln in the election of 1860. They were averse to change, and in many cases were opposed to emancipation of blacks, as well as to many other issues that would upset their accustomed ways of living on the land. But they were deeply affected by the Civil War, and many were involved in the fighting, including Benjamin Avery Posten.

The authors of *Damn Dutch* write that the Pennsylvania Dutch were not only strong fighters for the Union, but that their experiences of the war may have been different because of the strong identity resulting from their shared cultural background. Despite four years of war, they were able to "maintain a unique cultural awareness while at the same time embracing a larger American identity which the war helped strengthen."[28]

By that standard, Benjamin Avery may well have come away from the war feeling not only more deeply rooted in his own culture and traditions, but also more closely identified with America. If so, it would be no surprise that he may have looked to a new start in the Ozarks, in the very heartland of America, as a place to make his stake.

POSTEN IN THE OIL BUSINESS: BEFORE THE WAR

MONTHS BEFORE HIS enlistment in the army, Benjamin had struck out from home in order to find work. Oil had been discovered elsewhere in Pennsylvania, and he heard they were hiring and provided a decent wage. He may have realized that war was drawing closer and that soon he would be called into service. There was still time to earn some extra money in preparation for harder times to come. He traveled to Oil Creek in January of 1862 to get a job and discovered that Oil Creek was not a pretty town. Living conditions were deplorable.

It is often forgotten that the first oil boom in America happened in Pennsylvania. The area eventually lost its prominence as a producer of oil to such places as Texas, but it had the honor of being first.

Drake and Company first successfully drilled for oil in August 1859 at a site near Titusville, Pennsylvania. The resulting oil boom has been compared to the discovery of gold in California.[29] The rustic farming country rapidly changed as leases for oil were quickly secured and new towns appeared on the horizon almost overnight. What had once been a simple, quiet rural area because a noisy, bustling place. Wells were sprouting up all over the place, creating the need for lots of machinery to bring up the oil. Once it was out of the ground, the oil had to be transported to the refiners, and horses and wagons were the means of transport. The dirt trails became muddy when it rained and had to be widened to allow traffic to flow. So deep was the mud that the horses had to work beyond their capacity and were often stuck in it. A vivid description of the scene was provided by newspaperman J.H. Bone, a reporter for the *Cleveland Herald*:

> Oil City at last, Oil City, with its one long, crooked and bottomless street. Oil City, with its dirty houses, greasy plank sidewalks, and fathomless mud. Oil City, where horsemen ford the street in from four to five feet of liquid filth, and where the inhabitants wear knee-boots as part of in-door equipment. Oil City, which will give the dirtiest place in the world three feet advantage and then beat it in depth of mud. Oil City, where weary travelers think themselves blest if they can secure their claim to six feet of floor for the night, and where the most favored individual accepts with grateful joy the offer of half a bed and the twentieth interest in a bed-room.[30]

Benjamin felt fortunate to share a crowded shack with a few friends. He was glad to have a job, although the real money was to be had in real estate, as the prices were rising dramatically. Later, shrewd businessmen like John D. Rockefeller and Jabez Bostwick would put together plans to monopolize and make fortunes out of this oily substance. But it took workers like Benjamin to get it out of the ground and process it. Hard work though it was, the finding of oil was big news, and promised jobs for those willing to endure the terrible conditions under which one had to live and work.

When Benjamin wrote Mary in January 1862, he was staying in one of the shantytowns and daily inhaling air permeated with oil, dealing with constantly oily hands, and walking daily in the legendary mud. It was dangerous work, too. The wells could catch fire. The first one Drake drilled was short-lived before it burned to the ground. Despite all that, Benjamin made no complaints, made no reference at all to the hardships. He had a job. He was making money. That was good enough for now.

One night, late, after his roommates had gone to sleep in their too-crowded room, he sat down and penned a letter to Mary as he would often do in the days ahead when he was away from home as a soldier:

> *I have been working every day since I came to Oil Creek.*
> *I have been working for William most of the time for 50*
> *cents a day, some days 75, some 1.00, some 1.50 and I*
> *worked one night from midnight til morning for 1.00. I*
> *have not got all my money yet, but I will send you some...*

The letter was a direct response to the one he had just received from Mary. She had written urging her husband to "try send a little money." She needed money to purchase a few things, as she was not able to sell enough butter to buy groceries. Mary also brought her husband up to date about the children:

> *This morning Sady had a bad cold but she is better. She*
> *is full of mischief as ever. Mary is well and growing fine.*

Even though Benjamin was working, he was not at home,

and even now that was an extra burden. Mary Ellen had gone to other family members for help.

I could not get a boy to stay and do the work. Sarah is staying with me and she does all the out door work and most of the work in the house. Father attends to chopping the wood...

News from home, but the bottom line, which she reiterated in her closing, was that she needed some money.

Financial need was what had taken him to Oil Creek, and he was happy to oblige her request, knowing the situation was about to drastically change.

The war was getting closer to home, and there were growing threats as Confederate troops advanced toward Washington D.C. Clearly alarmed at the prospect of General Robert E. Lee marching into the nation's capital, President Lincoln called for 300,000 more troops. Whatever the desire and need for additional income might have been, the President's call was enough to take Posten home, where he did not linger long before he enlisted in the 140th Regiment.

Posten was about to engage in what has been called "the rich man's war, the poor man's fight." Early in the war, volunteers were rewarded with a $100 bonus, which was attractive to poor families. The Militia Act of 1862 made the states responsible for drafting men if they did not meet their quotas. In 1863 Congress passed the first conscription law and the sign-up reward rose to $300. In addition, the Conscription Act allowed anyone who could pay $300 to be excused from the draft call: a man could be permanently exempted by hiring someone to take his place. The practice of paying for a substitute was taken up by many of the more well-to-do, including

John D. Rockefeller, who was already engaged in the profitable oil industry, and J.P. Morgan, who made huge profits providing war materials. Grover Cleveland, who would later become President, also chose to purchase a substitute and continue to engage in his profitable legal practice. [31]

President Lincoln, though not eligible for the draft, sought to set an example for those choosing not to serve by purchasing his own substitute.[32]

POSTEN AND THE CIVIL WAR

MANY MEN WHO identified as Pennsylvania Dutch joined the fight to save the Union, especially as war came close to home, and Benjamin Posten was among them. It was well enough for the young man to follow his heart and duty and go away to fight for his country, but Mary was left with the immense responsibility of running the entire household as well as taking care of the farm. The couple had been married only three years and already had two daughters, Sarah (Sady), born in 1860, and Mary (Molly), born in 1861. But there was no stopping either the war or young Benjamin's determination. In September 1862, along with others from Mercer County, he enlisted in the 140th Pennsylvania Infantry Regiment, Company B, and was soon given his uniform, which has been described in some detail by writer Robert Stewart:

> The outfit provided by the government for the rank and file in those days consisted of a dark blue blouse, light blue trousers, a smart look frock coat with brass buttons for dress parade and special occasions, a cotton or mixed wool and cotton shirt, a suit of underwear, a forage cap, stout broad-soled shoes and a blue overcoat with a heavy cape.[33]

In a memorable photo, Posten proudly poses for the camera, smartly dressed in his new uniform and displaying his full beard—perhaps inspired by Lincoln himself, who had grown facial hair just before his inauguration.

This was an exciting time for the young recruits. All were leaving their occupations as farmers, mechanics, shopkeepers, and college students for a fight that would pose great danger to themselves and inflict hardship on their families back home. None had military training. The group was described, nonetheless, as a "glorious regiment, composed of noble men."[34]

When the 140th Regiment received orders on September 9, they assumed they would be sent to the front lines. They waited patiently until 4 a.m. for the train to arrive, still having no word on their destination. Several hours after they boarded the train it stopped at Parton Station in Maryland and they were ordered to make camp. To their surprise and general disappointment they were then informed that this was their assignment, to guard the important rail station, for the next three months. The young men had been fired up for what they considered real fighting, and this was not it. Guard duty could be quite boring, as soldier and writer Robert Stewart, who was stationed there with Posten, wrote:

> Aside from guard duty, our time is fully occupied at Parton in company and battalion drill and the ordinary route of camp life.[35]

The assignment at Parton gave the raw recruits time to hone their skills and probably helped save some lives when bloody conflict eventually came, but for now they were disappointed. They also did not like the antiquated rifles they were furnished with (the new Springfield rifles would not come until months later). The conditions were miserable, and when they could, the soldiers purchased food items such as pies and cakes from vendors who worked the camp. Those treats were a great relief from the bread and beans that were their main rations. Even though they were not confronted with flying bullets, men in the camp were still sick and dying, primarily from malaria and typhoid.

Posten too had been energized by the prospects of war, and fit in well with the other recruits. Whatever inner conflicts he may have had, and despite a diversity of opinion about the war among the Pennsylvania Dutch, he felt strongly attached to American ideals and to the concept of a united nation, and he scorned those who would secede from the Union. He stated his own reasons for joining the fight in a poem he sent to his wife in October 1862, just a month after joining the regiment and while stationed on guard duty at Parton Station in Maryland.

The Brave Soldier
Now my dear friends I am going away to a fight for my country.
How long shall I stay? Why I've no feeling of dread.
I'll stay till rebellion is crushed out and dead.
And I assure you that it will not be long
Our generals are true, for our army is strong.
Arms, they are mighty, and able to save.
Union forever and dig traitors a grave.
We have enlisted for a term of three years.
To go boldly forth to battle with cheers.
To rush on the foeman, wherever they are, to drive, take and slaughter.
And give utter despair.

Tis true there is no mercy by rebels is shown.
And now we will pay them in coin of their own.
It will not be in darkies, whom they call slaves.
But in digging and filling confederate graves.
When this is accomplished and rebellion is put down
then
I will haste to my friends and sweet home. You will hear
The steps of a soldier in the yard or front.
And a cheer for the Union and close of the war.

While the young man's poem is filled with youthful swagger, it is a good representation of the young men in the regiment, who were utterly naive about the war, the realities of bloody battle, the horrors they would face, how long the war might last, and how many among them would be wounded, lose their limbs, or die. There is little doubt that Posten's enthusiasm waned as the terrible war took its toll. That first assignment consisting of guard duty and drill was hardly an adequate representation of what was to come. The war was not brief, as his poem predicted, and before Benjamin was mustered out of service three years later, he would see the horror of war on many fronts, including the Battle of Chancellorsville, and the deadliest battle of them all, Gettysburg, in July 1863.

It had already been a cold winter when in December of 1863 the regiment received orders to go to Washington, D.C. Upon their arrival, they marched through Baltimore buoyed by bands playing and enthusiastic crowds waving flags and handkerchiefs, singing their praises.

There is no record of Posten's personal reaction to Gettysburg, but much has been written about that battle. The figures enumerating those who died or were wounded may vary, but all agree that the carnage was astounding and that it was one of the bloodiest battles in the history of North America.

A few days after the battle a reporter from the *Daily Patriot and Union* newspaper went to the scene and was astounded at what he saw. He wrote that "It was the saddest commentary of human ambition it has ever been our lot to behold."[36] Days after the battle, bodies had not been buried. The battlefield was cluttered with evidence of struggle: muskets, blankets, and articles of clothing were everywhere, and many dead horses were among the ruin. The stench was carried miles from the battlefield.

There were many more battles to be fought. The war continued year after year, and by January 1865, Benjamin Posten, like others who had participated in the long fight, was feeling exhausted by war. Mary too was weary of struggling to make ends meet at home while her husband was constantly in danger. Benjamin was now stationed with the 140th Regiment as it took part in the Siege of Petersburg, Virginia. General Ulysses Grant and his forces had built trenches around parts of Richmond, Virginia, and Petersburg. The railway lines brought in crucial supplies to General Robert E. Lee and the Confederate army, as well as to the citizens of Richmond. Many raids and battles were fought, largely utilizing trench warfare, until Union troops were finally successful in cutting off supplies. At that point, General Lee retreated from the city, leading to the surrender at Appomattox Court House.

January 9, 1865, was a bleak day, cold and rainy. Everyone involved in the siege was tired of the rain. Another soldier, Octave Brusco, who was also taking part in the battle, kept a diary and made a note on that day: "Rained hard all night and all day. Went out after wood at 10 a.m. and got wet through. Did not feel good all the rest of the day."

Benjamin too was experiencing the effects of the rain, and he was feeling lonely, suffering from boredom, and longing for home. Stuck on guard duty at 2 a.m., he sat down to write Mary a letter. The young soldier was fortunate there were no incidents that night, because his attention was clearly elsewhere. First, he wanted to clear up a misunderstanding. Despite her belief to the contrary, he was in fact sending her letters on a regular basis. He went on to list the exact days the letters were posted. After providing what he considered proof, he added, "So I think I am not in any debt for letters." He then encouraged her to double check the dates of the letters she had received, and confirm the information he had provided. There is little doubt that Benjamin Posten was a stickler for detail.

The young father was concerned, as usual, about the children, especially Sady, who had been ill, and also about his wife, who had to do all the work at home. "Sorry that you have to run around to harvest hay, but I hope by the time another winter comes around that I will be there to attend to such matters myself." That was no doubt Mary's hope as well.

The late-night letter continued: "I have not any money yet, and you wanted to know whether I wanted socks and gloves. I would like to have about two pair of socks and some tomatoes, but I have the same pair of gloves you sent last winter." Then there was the matter of sending him food. "If you send any tomatoes you must put them in a stone jar but you best not send any canned fruits for such stuff is apt to get destroyed, for they think, at headquarters, that it is whiskey and they are sure apt to punch holes in the cans to see what is in them… but you can send such as dried cakes, apples, and such…"

Packages from home were always welcome, but as much as Benjamin appreciated what Mary would send, he was not going hungry. At times he was fed quite well. As fellow soldier and diarist Robert Stewart observed, there was plenty to eat on Thanksgiving Day. "… an abundant supply of good things was sent to the troops for general distribution," he wrote, including turkeys, hams, cans of fruit, apples, grapes, and lots of cakes. "Suffice it to say that every mess in the Army of the Potomac had a feast of good things, similar to our own, from a supply that seemed to be inexhaustible."[37]

The guard-duty watch was coming to an end, and the sleepy solider started to close the letter, wishing Mary and the children a good night's sleep. But he was not quite ready to break the connection he got from just writing the letter.

"It is still raining and has been thundering now… and it looks as though it might continue for a week." Then he adds a comment about the war itself. "There was a man shot in our Division last Friday for desertion. The Rebs are still coming over pretty near every night and I hope they will continue to come until they are all within our lines. Colonel Rodgers is now in command of the Regt. and we all like him much better than some that had command."

The solder Benjamin referred to was Michael Wert, with the 184th Regiment, who was executed January 6, 1865, by firing squad, only days before the letter was written. Although Benjamin likely did not know the soldier personally, the man had enlisted out of Pennsylvania around the time Benjamin entered the army.

There were, at this date in the war, a large number of desertions from the Confederate Army as soldiers came into Union territory to surrender. That trend became more pronounced with each Union victory as the South's eventual loss of the war became more apparent. One general described what was occurring every night during the siege in the winters of 1864 and 1865: They "… crept through their picket lines, dropped their arms, and came to us as individuals in squads, amounting in the aggregate to thousands."[38]

The deserters from the Confederate Army may have seemed to Benjamin a hopeful sign that the war was winding down and would soon be won in the Union's favor. He may not have known that during the course of the war, there were twice as many desertions from the Union ranks. The reasons for desertion were many, including boredom, lack of interest in the mission, or weariness from battle. It is also true that many soldiers, like Benjamin, were from poor families, and many were farmers who were understandably worried about their own families who were struggling in their absence. As the war progressed there were added inducements to enemy soldiers to desert: the Union began to allow deserters from the South to pledge allegiance to the United States and then return to their homes. Later they upped the bounty by offering transportation and even the purchase of war-related equipment.

At one point, desertion by Union troops got so bad that Lincoln issued an order allowing all deserters amnesty if they would return to their ranks by a given date. Although the traditional punishment for desertion was death, the huge number of deserters had made that an impractical solution. Even so, in the instance Benjamin mentioned in his letter to Mary, the soldier in his division had indeed received the ultimate punishment.

As the rain continued to fall, accompanied by the sound of thunder, Benjamin had one more comment to add before he closed the letter. "I am going to put a ring in the letter for you.

It is one made out of a Rebel Shell and I want you to take good care of it till I come home." That said, the homesick soldier signed off in his usual manner, "Your loving husband."

The practice of turning Rebel shells into rings was exercised by a number of soldiers. One writer from the 140th Regiment wrote that some of those rings would sell for as much as three dollars, and observed that on November 11, 1864, "A shell lit in the tube where a soldier was washing his handkerchief, whereupon one of the bystanders swore he'd have it made into rings before the johnnies could shoot another."[39]

Since Benjamin was stationed at that encampment when he wrote about the ring in his January 1885 letter to Mary, it is possible he was the bystander the author wrote about in his diary. It is a pleasing thought to imagine Benjamin surrounded by his comrades, men he had come to know well and trust through the rigors of war, strike a word of humor and make that comment about the ring. A possibility, but it is more likely the soldier quoted someone else, and that Benjamin was simply another soldier engaging in this popular activity.

On October 17, 1864, just a few months before Benjamin wrote the January letter, President Lincoln, Secretary Stanton, and General Grant had visited the troops. They "rode along the lines and were accorded a hearty greeting by the troops, who, with the exception of those needed for garrison duty in the trenches, were assembled in rear of the works."[40] Unless Benjamin had the misfortune of being assigned to guard duty on that particular day, he may well have gotten a good look at President Lincoln, who was assassinated six months later on April 15, 1865.

The signs were looking good; the war's end seemed near at hand. Soon Benjamin would be going home. But for many others this was not the case. Jessie M. Vogan, also a member of Company B the 140th Regiment, and married to Mary Posten's sister, Sarah, wrote Mary in November of 1864 while he was hospitalized at the Lincoln General Hospital in Washington, D.C., one of the largest military hospitals built by the army to take care of Civil War casualties.

The wounded man wondered why other relatives, in particular his own wife, had not been writing. Had she gotten his letters? "It seems as though all the folks have forgotten me its pretty near right. And I don't feel very well anyway," he wrote. Vogan went on say he was pleased he could at least correspond with his sister-in-law, and he promised to see her soon. "Tell Sady and Mary Uncle Jessie would be at there house to see them." He wrote that he expected to return to his company within a few weeks. The forgotten soldier did recover enough from his wounds to return to combat, but his promise to see his nieces would not be fulfilled, as he was to die on April 7, 1865, at the Battle of High Bridge, just two days before Lee's surrender at Appomattox on April 9, 1865.

The war ended less than three months after Benjamin's January letter to Mary. The 140th Pennsylvania Regiment was active in the war until it ended with Lee's surrender. In May of 1865, Benjamin Posten, who had been promoted to corporal in October of 1864, along with thousands of other weary soldiers, was mustered out of service.

Benjamin returned home to his family and took up again the work of farming. He would remain in Pennsylvania for a few more years and Mary would have three more children: Luella in 1866, Charles in 1868, and Bessie May in 1870. But a big change was soon to occur; a plan to move to a new location was slowly taking form in Benjamin's mind.

TO THE OZARKS

WITHIN MONTHS OF Bessie May's birth, the family made their way to Missouri, eventually to settle in Pulaski County in the Ozarks. They moved at a pivotal time in the history of the area. The 1889 *History of Pulaski County* reported that the advent of the railroad in 1869–70 had marked the dividing line between two epochs, from a place that was mostly pastoral to one with "urban tastes."[41]

Writer Milton D. Rafferty observes that the earliest American settlers in the Ozarks came mostly from the South and were of Scotch-Irish descent. Immigrants that came after the Civil War were a different breed. Entrepreneurs, capitalists of various ilk, builders, traders, government officials, and Civil War veterans came from different parts of the country seeking to build homes and towns. In comparison to the earlier settlers, they were "urbane, educated and progressive."[42]

The years between 1867 and 1877 saw a huge influx of new arrivals to Missouri. Whether they knew it or not, the Posten family was embarking not only on a journey to a new place, but also into a new and different flow of history.

Once again, the reasons why someone got the itch to move on, to leave behind most of what they owned and all those they were acquainted with can only be guessed. Perhaps things were not going well for Benjamin in Pennsylvania, or he simply wanted to be far from the battlefields where he had once fought. Then again, it was an age when many families were moving west. The movement itself may have seized his imagination. He was still relatively young, in his early thirties, and even though he had a family to consider, which made any major move challenging, once the notion got into his head to head for new territory, Missouri became his chosen destination.

Benjamin knew something of Missouri from other relatives who had gone there already. As a Union patriot, he was not deterred by the history of the state or of Pulaski County itself. Although the state was not part of the Confederacy, it was a slaveholding state. The 1860 slave census indicated there were fifty-six slaves in Pulaski County, six of whom resided in Waynesville.[43]

During the war, in the spring of 1861, a Confederate flag was raised at the Waynesville Court House and then quickly taken down by Union troops who restored the stars and stripes. It was evidence of how divided the state was during the war, when it was essentially fighting its own civil war, neighbor against neighbor. Fewer than 500 troops had officially joined the fray, and they were fairly equally divided between the Union and the Confederacy. In the presidential election of 1865, Lincoln received only seven votes from Pulaski County. The majority cast their votes for the southern candidate, indicating that a large portion of the county regarded their best interests as more akin to slaveholding states than the Union.[44]

The Civil War in Missouri consisted primarily of guerrilla raids and skirmishes. One incident involved a minister by the name of Calloway Manes, a Union sympathizer who let his opinions be known in his weekly sermons. This display of Union favoritism angered others in the community, and in particular a group known as the Bushwhackers who often demonstrated their allegiance to the Confederacy in the form of violent action. The Bushwhackers warned Reverend Manes to stop preaching in support of the Union, and when he failed to do so, they took action, appearing at his house one night and shooting him as he stood in his doorway. When they saw that he was not yet dead, the invaders went into his home and forced his daughters to hold a candle while they finished the job. [45]The house where this event took place is still standing at this writing, and is located just outside the city limits of Richland, Missouri.

Although there were no major battles fought in Missouri, the war greatly impacted parts of the state, including Pulaski County. It created devastating effects on the people, the buildings, and livestock. Some residents, seeing the turmoil coming, had left previous to the war. They returned to find their houses burned and their farm animals gone. The land had not been managed and was overgrown. In Waynesville, the Old Stagecoach Stop that had once served as a tavern was one of the few remaining buildings. Many residents decided not to return, and their absence created room for new immigrants. [46]

Southwest Missouri made a concerted effort to attract a new population. In 1865 the General Assembly passed a law that created a State Board of Immigration. Newspapers throughout the state advertised to attract new landowners. *The Springfield Missouri Patriot* promised fertile lands, a healthy climate, running streams for the benefit of livestock, short winters, and cheap land. [47] Real estate agents were hard at work as well, though their interest was clearly profit-related. The railroads pitched in, at times offering discount fares for potential buyers as they needed to sell much of the extra land they owned.[48] Posten and his neighbors back in Pennsylvania had seen the ads and heard the claims of good land in Missouri. They had surely also learned that after the war, parts of the Ozarks resembled the wild frontier, with outlaws roaming the area. On the other hand, there were lots of new people moving in, and these were mostly people who just wanted to live, till the land, and build communities. Things were settling down. And the word of abundant game in the forest and fish in the streams, especially in the Gasconade and Piney Rivers, was also a big enticement.

This fit in perfectly with the Pennsylvania Dutch culture from which Benjamin and Mary Ellen had sprung. The tenets of religious freedom, emphasis on family and rural life, and the ability to live their own way without interference all helped make the isolation of the Ozarks particularly inviting.

Considering all the benefits, the greatest incentive, the final attraction that removed any doubts, was the factor that brought many others to the area: free land. The Homestead Acts passed in 1862 and 1864 were an impetus for people moving to Missouri. The act stipulated that in order to be eligible for up to 160 acres, an applicant had to meet certain qualifications: he must be head of a family, at least twenty-one years of age, and a citizen, and have not joined in the fight against the Union. Posten scored on every count.

Even so, there were obstacles, which Benjamin's father-in-law, William Parkinson Dean, indicated in a letter to his son dated June 8, 1870. Dean made reference to a conversation he had had with Benjamin and warned his son, who had already gone to Missouri, to be on the lookout for "gougers": "I don't want you nor any other man to buy where the title cannot be made good," the elder Dean warned. He wanted to go west as well, but he was deeply discouraged about the reports he was hearing about deceptive land deals. He was in a bad state. "We are almost out of heart and barely know what to do," he wrote. He was also discouraged about the reports he had heard that the good land was already taken. Life was not going well. "There is persons here that would cheat me out of my skins if they can only get hold of me. I have hard times and sometimes I am so crazier i cannot hardly write a letter. Your mother says she will come when the rest come, but she says she don't want to come and not find you there," he lamented. He needed a definite answer. "Now we want to know whether it is worth while to come and can we all get homesteaded by coming."

In August of the same year, Dean was still in Pennsylvania working out details about getting to Missouri. He wrote to another son, James, who had moved to Missouri, wondering how he and his wife would make the trip. Sarah wasn't well and Dean wasn't feeling so great himself, although he had been helping other farmers with the harvest. That correspondence made it clear that Benjamin Avery Posten was already in Missouri but Mary Ellen and the children were still in Pennsylvania. "Your mother wants you if Avery [Benjamin] comes to send your carpet sack to carry her fine clothes and if you could fetch it yourself. I intend to sell on the 30 of August and then start as soon after we sell. Your mother says she is bound to go, hit or miss."

Finally, Dean and Sarah made the move, but Sarah died not long after they arrived in Pulaski County. Dean lived another ten years, dying in 1880 while living with his daughter Sarah and her husband, William Williams.

Benjamin Posten did make his big move despite whatever obstacles may have been in the way. He, Mary Ellen, and the children all arrived in Missouri and he took up his homestead near what would become Fairview Baptist Church.

The life of a homesteader was certain to be difficult. There was land to be cleared of trees and brush, fields to be tilled, and crops to be planted, and certainly a house had to be built. It was tough to make a living on the land, which was far from prime. It is likely that as the children grew, the family found ways to supplement their income. One such source of added income, subscribed to by many others at the time and a reasonable activity for the Posten family, was tie-hacking.

Steven Smith refers to an older Pulaski County resident who observed that much of the farmland in the Ozarks was of such poor quality that only a farmer who was fortunate enough to have fertile bottomland could make a living. Otherwise, a farmer had to make ties for the railroad, or as he put it, "make it in the timber."[49] For a period of time during the 1870s and beyond, the railroad was booming and in constant need of rails. Farmers, as well as professionals, cut the forest with impunity in the pursuit of tie-hacking, or making railroad ties. The ties were either rafted down the river or taken by ox or horse to the railroad. A good tie-hacker could make about thirty ties a day, which in the 1870s were selling for fifteen cents each.

Dick Johnson, a lifelong resident of the county and for years a barber in Richland, recalled the tie-hackers at the turn of the century. "I remember the tie haulers around here made the trip to Richland each day. One family had 17 kids and the man and wife would ride the tie wagon 15 miles to town each day with only eight or nine ties, then 15 miles back home on the running gears of that wagon. The lady would buy groceries with the money they got for the ties."[50]

Richland was a center for the tie-buying business in the

1880s. After being floated down the Gasconade, the ties were held in an eddy until they were hauled by wagon to the Hobert Tie Company in Richland, which paid five cents per tie.[51]

It is more than idle speculation to suggest that Benjamin Posten resorted to this available source of income. There is equally no doubt that his family sustained themselves in the same manners as most of the early pioneers.

The keyword for these homesteaders was self-sufficiency. They grew their own corn, sorghum, and wheat, and they tended large gardens with an abundance of vegetables. They also availed themselves of berries and nuts in season. The Posten family likely raised a few hogs, had chickens for eggs and meat, kept their own cows for milk and butter. They hunted the abundance of wild game and fished in the nearby rivers.

The Posten homestead was, according to authors York and York, part of the community known as Bloodland.[52] A quick internet search will reveal that "Bloodland is a ghost town in southern Missouri, surrounded by Ft. Leonard Wood."[53] In its day it was so much more, with far more substance than that brief definition indicates. While it was just in its formation when the Postens arrived, it later became a flourishing community with a number of stores and mills, a post office, churches, a cemetery, a school, and a tomato cannery. A photograph of the Bloodland School taken in 1909 indicates a number of children in attendance with the name of Posten who were probably the grandchildren of Benjamin Avery.[54] Even so, the whole town, the entire community, would be eliminated in the 1940s, erased from the earth and turned into a "ghost town" when all its residents were forcefully evicted with the establishment of Ft. Leonard Wood.[55]

Benjamin and Mary Ellen did not live to see the glory days

of the community, but in their time they saw an ever-growing area, new people moving in, businesses going up. There were also general merchandise stores in Waynesville, and with the coming of the railroad in 1869, the towns of Richland and Crocker, as well as others, were established. In Richland, some twenty years before the Clarks made their entry, one could find a grocery, a school, and several other business concerns. Richland was also a source for media: newspapers. There was the short-lived *Rising Sun* in 1869, and the *Richland Sentinel* was active in 1870 and '71. The *Richland Cyclone* appeared in 1885 and was later transformed into a Republican paper, the only one in the county.[56]

Waynesville was already the center for business and government in Pulaski County. There was a grocery, a blacksmith, and even a lawyer. Just before the Civil War an inn was built across from the courthouse. It was later a bar and finally a stagecoach stop. Remarkably, it was not destroyed by the war, and is currently a tourist attraction.

Towns like Richland and Waynesville were a great resource for the newcomers and essential for meeting the needs of a growing population. These villages were important to people who lived in the area, but to many outsiders they were hardly worthy of notice and were of no importance. Steve Smith quotes diarist Benjamin F. McIntyre, who stated that Waynesville was little more than "a place for horse racing, quarrels & fights and where bad whiskey and poor tobacco is for sale at reasonable prices."[57] Smith quotes another federal soldier, Chester Barner, as saying the schoolhouse looked like it had been "mortgaged to a flock of sheep which had evidently occupied it unmolested for some time." The postmaster had evidently converted the post office "into a whiskey shop and tavern and was doing a thriving business."[58]

Even if outsiders with little vision were not impressed, things were changing in the Ozarks, and the railroad was playing a large part. It provided a great vehicle for commerce and transportation of goods and people and stimulated the growth of the area, but it did not offer much help for day-to-day travel for people who lived and worked in the rural territory. Travel was mostly by horse and wagon, if not on foot. The old Indian and animal trails, while good for walking, were not suitable for horse and wagon, so trees had to be felled, paths widened, and rocks pulled out of the way. A certain property of travel in these byways in the days of Benjamin Avery was dust in the summer and mud in the winter—or whenever it rained.

There were few roads worthy of the name when the Posten family arrived in Pulaski County. One route known as the old Houston road did go from Waynesville to Houston, Missouri; later, Highway 17 covered much of the same route. But roads that crossed the area would need bridges, and in 1889 there were still no bridges in Pulaski County. Transport across rivers was by way of ferries and fords. There were two ferries that worked the Gasconade, and twenty-nine fords. Another fifteen fords were found on the Big Piney.[59]

Charles Ousley, who lived in Crocker, was the first Pulaski County citizen to purchase an automobile. The year was 1912. Benjamin Avery and Mary Ellen Posten had already passed from the scene, but not so their children. One local resident recalled going a quarter of mile to Ben Posten's house for the sole purpose of watching a car pass along on the highway.[60] Ben Posten Jr., just two years older than his brother, Martin King, had married Alice Crossland in 1896, fathered ten children, and was to die in 1932.

Although the arrival of the automobile would help bring about major change, in the early days not everyone agreed these new machines were a good idea. Oma Hensley Willits, a long-time resident of the area, recalled that for some reason the early automobiles were locally referred to as "jitneys," and she remembered her father warning the children, "You children stay out of those Jitneys. I will be glad when they stop making them because a lot of people are going to get killed by those things."[61]

The local residents did, however, take a fancy to the automobile and nearly half of them owned one by the early 1930s. That and the earlier introduction of the railroad, the later advent of electricity, the World Wars, and the creation of Ft. Leonard Wood, as well as the all-imposing Great Depression, together exercised a great influence on the descendants of Benjamin Avery Posten.

The early residents of the Ozarks in Pulaski County were isolated in many respects, but not all. True, they mainly lived on farms, some long distances apart, and roads and means of transportation could be an issue. They were indeed remote from the outside world. But residents tended to fend for themselves and help each other out, and they managed to socialize well enough.

Robert Lincoln Barlow, a longtime resident of the area, kept a diary and had a farm near the Clarks. His diary entry of September 30, 1893, observes that he "Went to Mr. Posten's and traded for an oxen." He added that Ben Posten, son of Benjamin Avery and in his early twenties at the time, had spent the night.[62] Years later, in 1901, Barlow wrote that Carl Clark had come home with his son, Roscoe. That same week, he noted, Mr. and Mrs. Clark came to his house after church.

As the diary goes on to verify, there were frequent sleepovers by both relatives and friends. It was not uncommon for people to come by after church. Life was not without entertainment and amusement, either. Barlow writes that he is "Getting ready for tonight. Had a big time at the entertainment. Made over 18.00. Mr Chambers and Blanche, John David, Mary Carer, Sam Rollins, and Kate stayed all night (also Albert). Had a lot of fun. Did not sleep until broad daylight in the morning."[63]

The contents of the Barlow diary are a great reflection of what life was like in the late nineteenth century in rural Missouri. One of the interesting characteristics of that life was the extent of interaction with other members of the community. There were social events, including church on Sunday. There were frequent visits from neighbors for sharing of meals, trading of livestock, and sharing of a work project.

Barlow's busy life, in additional to teaching school, included sundry activities: going to church, butchering hogs, making jelly, doing the laundry, fishing and hunting with friends, working in the garden, going to the circus, attending a program of songs, and traveling to Richland and Waynesville. Once, he writes with what appears a touch of humor, "Winnie and some of the town scalawags went to Jim Sailings to a shindig."[64]

Residents of the Ozarks may have been remote from the rest of the world, but certainly not from each other. The area was well off the radar of popular destinations until much later, when tourism made its mark in the area. It was the very nature of the isolation of the Missouri Ozarks that attracted the Posten family and helped create the character of Benjamin Avery and Mary Ellen's descendants; it nurtured a sense of both independence and cooperation with neighbors, and a great respect for the United States, while allowing them to maintain a skepticism about government in general.

Mabel Manes Mottaz characterized these early Ozarkians as people who based their morals on "immutable values of the Bible. They believed in truth, honesty, humor, loyalty to one's home, family, neighbors, and country."[65] Those traits surely rang true for many, with one important caveat. These pioneers were typically fiercely independent, suspicious of government and any person or institution which might attempt to change their beliefs or move them in any direction they were not ready to go. They chose this place not because of its prime farming land, which it was not, unless they were lucky enough to get property with a river bottom. Earlier settlers looking for rich farmland had bypassed the Ozarks' rocky, less fertile soil in favor of the rich lands of Oregon and California. But the land was cheap, and it was unpopulated enough to allow one to feel he was not crowded.

Cultural geographer Carl O. Sauer, writing in the 1920s, concluded that the Ozarks, including Pulaski County, was settled last by certain pioneers "in part because of their poverty, but principally because of their isolation."[66] These settlers had little desire to be part of the larger world, and were glad to find a location remote enough for them to create and celebrate their own culture.

Steven Smith concisely sums up the character of these early pioneers:

> *The culture of the Ft. Leonard Wood people was a culture of simplicity, self-sufficiency, strong kin and community ties, suspiciousness of outsiders, and familiarity with*

the land. Their anti-authoritarianism and their direct
daily struggle with the landscape brought a true freedom
unprecedented in the history of once-free America. This
freedom was bought at a high price. But on the plateau,
success or failure was theirs alone to find or endure. This
is the meaning of Ozark isolation: it was the freedom of
self-determination.[67]

Religion, with the local church as a central gathering place, served to bring people together to socialize as well as worship. Benjamin and Mary Ellen were both members of Fairview Baptist Church, which was less than a mile from their home. The church was first organized in December of 1883. In 1892 and 1899, Benjamin was appointed to committees on Sabbath Schools and Home Missions, respectively. In 1901 he held the office of Ministerial Educator.

The Smith Valley Association was held at Fairview Baptist Church in 1890, and the name of the organization was changed to Pulaski County Baptist Association. During the 1880s there was a series of protracted revival meetings, and the church membership grew; church members were busy donating labor to build the new church building.[68]

The protracted revival meeting was common among churches. A revival would take place once or twice a year and have no specific end date. Those who lived in the backwoods may have been far removed from the vices often considered on display in big cities, but the people were reminded constantly that evil dwelt among them, that sin was in everyone, and that there was a need not only for repentance, but also for reaffirmation to the ways of God as described in the Bible and interpreted by the preachers of the day.

The church served a very important social function. This was the place you could go not only to refresh your spiritual life, but also to greet your neighbors and find out what was going on in their lives. Oma Hensley Willits recalls that church was also the place for romance. The boys would pick out the girls they wanted to walk home and form a line just inside the front door of the church in an effort to encourage their selections to come with them. This plan worked both ways, as the whole thing was like "passing a firing squad"; the girls had equal opportunity to reject the lads they did not care to be with.[69]

The evangelical churches, such as the one Benjamin Avery attended, expressly forbade many popular diversions such as dancing, card playing, gambling, and consumption of alcoholic beverages. Church membership was taken seriously and violators of social mores risked censure and even withdrawal from church fellowship. Even failure to attend services for too long a time without reasonable excuse could incur disciplinary action from a church committee. The committee might first bring the accusations of wrongdoing to the church member at home, and then provide them opportunity to ask for forgiveness, which, if requested, was most often granted. In 1885 a committee from the Waynesville Baptist Church visited a member and his wife who were accused of using profanity and engaging in other forbidden conduct. Since the wife did not appear for judgment, the evidence was considered conclusive; she was deemed guilty and lost church membership. In other cases, membership was withdrawn from a woman for dancing and from a man for drinking.[70]

The church services themselves provided a source of entertainment. Some preachers were known for their eloquence and their ability to capture and keep the attention of an audience. Their sermons were far from boring. This was especially true of the visiting evangelists who came to conduct the revival meetings; some of these got reputations akin to star quality. They preached spirited sermons documented with true life stories and filled with emotion, and were greeted with inspiring emotional outbursts from the crowd. Shouting, waving of the hands, "amens," testimonials, and other forms of direct interaction with the sermon were not uncommon.[71]

In 1905 the association meeting mourned the deaths of both Mary Ellen and Benjamin Avery, who died just three months after his wife's demise. By the time the church building was dedicated in 1908, all senior members of the Posten-Bostwick family who had participated in the life of the church had passed from the scene.

THE WILL

Soon after Mary Ellen's death, Benjamin Avery realized it was time he took care of the legal matters that would arise in regard to his own death. Perhaps he was already ill, or maybe he just had a feeling his days were numbered. He sat down at the kitchen table, grief-stricken but determined to write down his final thoughts and decisions about who would inherit his property.

On Thursday, May 7, 1905, he hooked up the team and drove to Richland, where he signed his final will and testament in front of witnesses. That day was full of sorrow and memories. Mary Ellen had died just three days before. Her grave was still fresh, even if the flowers that covered it had started to wither. Her death was the biggest loss of his life. They had gone through much together. He recalled his youthful pride posing in his new uniform, then marching off to face the harsh realities of war; he remembered fondly how the letters from Mary Ellen had helped sustain him during that trying time, and he smiled as he remembered the joy of returning home to his family. Then there was anxiety and uncertainty, as well as excitement, as the family planned and completed the move to the Missouri Ozarks. Although the work on the homestead had been difficult, the land belonged to him and Mary Ellen and they had raised a family there. There was satisfaction in that.

Benjamin had changed much. Now stooped, his body was often in pain. The black beard he had grown at the beginning of the war so many years ago was now entirely gray. He felt old that day. It was time to set things in order.

He wrote, in the customary manner, that he was of sound mind and memory, and also knew of the "uncertainty of life and the certainty of death." He wanted to be buried "in a Christian manner, according to the rights of the Missionary Baptist Church." The entire bulk of his estate—the house, the farm, and all its properties—would go to Artie Belle and Alice Blanche.

The grieving man believed he had good reason to make this decision, regardless of what some of the other potential heirs might think. For one thing, the two daughters, who were two of a set of triplets, the third of which died in infancy, were twenty-five years old and unmarried. If they did not marry the farm would at least provide them shelter and some income whether they kept or sold it. Also, Benjamin was in failing health and the two live-at-home daughters had taken over the duties of housekeeping and much of the farm work. They were his care-takers in his old age and deserved extra consideration.

Both daughters did eventually marry. Artie Belle wed William Gan not long after the will was signed. Alice married Lee Hatfield three years later in 1908. The signing of the will was well timed. This would be the man's last spring. Three months later, on August 18, 1905, at the age of sixty-five and at the very height of the heat and humidity of the Ozark summer, Benjamin Avery Posten died. He was buried beside Mary Ellen in the Fairview Cemetery, a short distance from the homestead.

The old house stood for many years a solitary ghost, long forgotten, abandoned and weathered, the lone structure in a field of grass. It looked as though a big gust of wind might blow it over, and it seemed surprising that its bare bones stood at all. In the year before his death, Ralph stopped his truck on the gravel road alongside the property, stepped over the barbwire fence, and walked out into the open field. He made a quick tour of the remaining skeleton of the house, paused briefly, returned to the truck, and drove away without saying a word. The remains of the building were finally demolished and hauled away during the 1990s.

THE RALPH AND VELMA
CLARK POSTEN STORY

TWINS VELMA RUBY and Verga Clark were born on March 19, 1919. The two enjoyed a special bond that lasted their entire life, although they often lived far apart. Already present in the household were their siblings Cora and Lewis. Fern, the youngest, would follow a few years later.

The Clarks of Pulaski County were a rural family of modest means. Although the farm was located far from a major city and some distance from the nearest town, they did have neighbors. Carl Clark, his brother Myrl, and their father Luverne all had adjoining farms. The Luverne Clark family was large and several other relatives were not far away.

The farm itself was located on what came to be known as the Bellefonte Loop, a gravel road just off old Route 66. It formed a loop that passed the Rollings Cemetery and a number of farms, including those belonging to Wellington Barlow; Herbert Barlow; Carl, Myrl, and Verette Clark; and finally curved around to the Joe Elam farm before connection again with Route 66. For many years the Barlows, Clarks, and Elams were the primary residents of the loop.[72]

Velma, like all the Clark children, walked two miles to the

Bellefonte School. All the children graduated from high school in Richland, which was a remarkable achievement in itself, given the family's financial status and the distance to Richland; it was the nearest high school but not an easy commute in that day. For that reason Velma and Verga rented an apartment in Richland for a while during high school; another expense, but further evidence of the importance this farm family put on education.

Life on the farm required hard work, and lots of it. Everyone was expected to participate. Even so, at least in Velma's memories, it was a good life, as she later expressed in a poem published in the *Richland Mirror.*

My Childhood Memories on the Farm
When I was a little girl
I lived on a farm,
With three sisters, and one brother.
A sweet dad and mother.
My dad tilled the ground
With two mules and a plow
While mother mostly stayed
In the kitchen to prepare
For us the best chow.
We would rise early
Always before dawn.
This was a rule
So we could get our chores done
Before walking two miles to school.
Our bedrooms were always warm in the winter.
They were upstairs you see.
Dad always had the wood stove going

90 degrees.
Our food prepared from our garden.
Our meat and milk from the farm.
We didn't use sprays
We feared no harm.
When we went to the market
I can hear it still.
The iron wheels on the wagon
Hitting all the rocks on the hills.
I have a twin sister.
So was double you see.
We always got the same thing.
I know it was a worry at sight.
But it always saved a fuss or a fight.
We were a happy family
Although times we didn't all agree.
We had sad times, good times.
Happy times, bad times.
But this happens in all families you see.
I don't have a movie of the times I can see.

The Clark twins stayed connected throughout their lives. There were visits, some joyous and others with a somber tone, as when Verga journeyed back from Santa Rosa, California, on a train that also conveyed the coffin of her sixteen-year-old daughter who died of cancer and was buried in the Hazelgreen Cemetery. Velma visited Verga when she was in failing health and living in an assisted living facility in Santa Rosa. They seldom made phone calls, but did correspond by mail. In earlier years, Verga sent care packages consisting of the clothes her children had outgrown. Sometimes the sisters reflected on the changes and transitions in their lives. On the eve of their fifty-ninth birthday, Verga wrote, "I can't believe we are in our late 50s. Can you? No, I don't feel so good a lot of the time."

In their youth the twins often dressed alike, and in a nostalgic letter Verga wrote when both were widows and Verga was living in a care center, she told her sister she loved her and planned to visit and attend their high school reunion. She added, "Let's get dresses like we did before." They did just that, purchasing identical patterned dresses to wear to the reunion. High school graduation had been an important achievement for both of them. They managed to finish school despite the obstacles they faced, and were proud to have done so.

Verga and Velma also dressed alike for their high school yearbook photos in 1936. Their maternal grandfather, Charles M. Daily, wrote a letter at that time to his granddaughter Cora, who was married to Lewis Posten and living in Woodlake, California. Charles wrote that he planned to visit Carl Clark "in blackberry time" and that he was pleased with the room his son, George, had built for him onto his home in Marshfield, Missouri. He appreciated the senior photos Velma and Verga had sent him and remarked, "they look fine." They did indeed; the Clark twins made an attractive pair.

Velma never thought of herself as a poet or a writer of any kind. She would have laughed at the very thought of such a thing. Still, deep inside, underneath all those roles she had to play as mother, wife, housekeeper, and factory worker, there was a creative spark that just had to come out from time to time, even though it never had the opportunity to flourish. Not only did she try her hand at poetry, she dared to have her work locally published. She was pleased to attend the class reunion and was inspired to write a poem to celebrate the occasion.

We Are The Class of 36
Forty-five years ago, we were
Active and full of glee.
But now we are some older
And have slowed down you see.
Our hair may have some silver
This is nature you see.
If we have our health and get about
That is mostly of our life throughout.
Our class of thirty-six
Was extra special
Extra special to me.
It included two sets of twins.
One set was my sister Verga and me.
In RHS we always had lots of fun.
But our good professor Mr. Tripp
Was always on the run.
We studied hard to make the score
But there were many times we needed to do more.
Our sponsor she was great to try to guide us through the
years.
We know there were many times
That she could have shed tears.
Our class was very small
A number of twenty-eight.
But we always had good teaching
To try and keep us strait.
Our school didn't have the problems that the schools
have today.
But we are sure, they would have been taken care of
In a good and proper way.

The sad time has come for us to say
We have lost four from our class as of today.
Its a happy time to meet our class of 36.
Just to see their smile.
We want to thank many of them
Who came for many a mile.

Velma and Ralph had grown up in adjoining communities in Baptist families, although they belonged to different churches. The two were aware of each other because Ralph's older brother, Lewis, and Velma's older sister, Cora, married in 1933. As early as May 1936, Fern, still in high school, wrote in her diary that Ralph was there for dinner. What the diary did not say was that he had shown up more than once intoxicated, and Carl had sent him away. It would be years before he and Velma married, and it was not likely love at first sight. Showing up drunk was not the way to impress Velma Clark.

The couple shared many common values. Both were from farm families that were impacted by the Great Depression. Ralph's youth had been more disadvantageous. For one thing, he came from a very large family that suffered more poverty. Mart Posten had lost the farm, as had so many others during those trying times. There were hints that Mart may not have been that ambitious, and yet the family needed to earn every penny they could just to survive, and that eliminated any prospect for Ralph to go to high school. Instead he immediately went to work for farmers after graduating from the eighth grade. Although in later life he would take responsible positions in the church and community and would start his own business, the lack of a higher education was a hindrance that affected him the rest of his life. Intelligent, with a fine mind, he sometimes felt frustrated at the lack of tools at his disposal; something that more education would have helped provide.

Ralph had been a sickly child who suffered from rheumatic fever. One of his sisters recalled that they'd had to carry the sick child around as he rested on a pillow. Though his life may have been difficult, that did not stop him from rigorously applying himself to work or from finding activities that brought him relaxation and joy for all of his life, and nothing did that more than hunting and fishing.

As a youth he hunted in the nearby forest, often in the same woods that his grandfather, who died before his birth, had also traversed. He also fished in the Gasconade, a waterway described as one of the most crooked rivers in the world. It meanders 280 miles, all within the confines of the state of Missouri, and finally converges with the Missouri River near the town of Gasconade.

In the 1930s, the Gasconade, along with other rivers, was targeted for dams that would have generated electricity and provided flood control. A dam would also have backed up the water and formed a lake that would have drastically changed the flow and natural beauty of the river, which in turn would have altered Ralph's lifetime of rich experience on that stream. The economic woes of the Great Depression caused plans for the damn to be scrapped, saving the river.[73] In time, other dams would be built; not on the Gasconade, but within an hour's drive. For others, the new lakes that resulted provided a wonderful resource for recreation of all kinds, but Ralph Posten had no interest in lakes. For him the Gasconade was the zenith of waterways, the only body of water on which he wanted to cast his boat.

In 1939, Ralph and Velma were just getting married and

making plans to move west. It was an exciting time for both. Velma had already spent some time in California after high school graduation, when as a single woman she went to stay with her sister Cora in Woodlake. While there she did various jobs to earn her keep, including babysitting. She liked to tell the story of an employer who tested her honesty by placing a silver dollar in plain view while she was away. Velma said, "I knew she was testing me." She, of course, did not touch that piece of silver.

By 1940 the couple had settled into their adopted state, residing in Lemon Cove in Tulare County, California, a place nestled in the foothills between Woodlake and Three Rivers. It was not by accident that they chose that location; it was near the home of Lewis and Cora Posten, as well as in the general vicinity where other relatives had emigrated, fleeing poverty and joblessness in the Ozarks.

From Woodlake it was only a few hours' drive to either Los Angeles or San Francisco, though the couple did not visit either city. They did visit Sequoia National Park, which was only a couple hours from their home, but seeing the sights was not a priority. It was difficult enough just to make a living. Ralph, then twenty-two years of age, did ranch work. His income according to the 1940 census came to $850 for the entire year. It was not a lot of money, but still good compared to what was available back in the Ozarks.

Augusta Black, another Pulaski County resident who had gone to California to find work during the same time period, wrote that her parents were amazed to hear she and her husband were making as much as thirty-five cents an hour at their California jobs.[74]

The couple was doing well enough. Ralph had work. Velma found jobs as she was able, but that came to a halt with the birth in June 1940 of Eddie, their first child, and the only one of their five children to be born in a hospital. Now they started to reconsider their priorities. They had just started a family and were missing the support of their parents and other relatives. They began to look back longingly at what they had left behind in their native state. The world was now at war and it looked as though the United States might soon get involved. The job situation in Missouri appeared more favorable. They concluded that the best option was to move back to the Ozarks.

It was not long after Eddie's birth that they returned. Ralph went back to farming, a pursuit necessary to economic survival but not one he truly relished. He was already convinced that times had changed and that a family could no longer make a living on a small farm. Only farmers on large established farms, with good land, often inherited, were able to make a living. Ralph knew he would eventually seek his livelihood elsewhere, even as he started his tenure on the farm.

The large farm on which the family became tenants was bordered by the Gasconade and featured a small one-bedroom house without electricity or running water. Their third child, Don, was born there on a February day so rain-drenched that the overflowing creek prevented the doctor from making a house call. A neighbor served as midwife. Cora had also been born at home after the family returned to Missouri, and in that case, Phoebe Posten performed the duties of midwife. Carl was later born in Richland, and David started life in the Clark house with some assistance from Dr. Myers.

In December of 1941, after the Japanese bombing of Pearl Harbor, the United States did enter the war and the draft went into action. Ralph was eventually notified to report for a physical for possible induction into military service. To get to the physical in St. Louis he needed to catch a bus on Route 66, a couple miles distant. Eddie, his young son, not really understanding what was going on, watched as his father took off walking across the field. At the end of that field Ralph had to roll up his trousers and ford the Gasconade at its low point, taking the final stretch of land that led to the highway.

The army physical resulted in a dire diagnosis that hit Ralph hard. It was a gloomy forecast. The doctor told the young farmer that his heart was enlarged and badly damaged. Not only was he unfit for military service, he was certain to have bad health consequences, and he was directed to return home and plan on doing no physical work for the remainder of his life. This was alarming news, but also a preposterous prescription as far as Ralph was concerned. He had little formal education and no trade outside farming. He also had a wife and two children to support. Disregarding the reports, he immediately went back to farming, and despite many years of various aspects of work that required physical exertion, as well as a vigorous outdoor recreational life, his heart was never an issue.

A TURKEY FIASCO

Farming was work Ralph felt compelled to do for the time being, but he had no intention of making it a lifelong pursuit. It so happened that the turkey business was flourishing after the war, and a turkey processing plant was built in Richland. Both Ralph and Velma were hired to work at the new facility and moved to Richland to be close to their jobs. They were happy just to have jobs, a theme that would be repeated several times over. They had learned that they could not take it for granted that work would always be available; the Depression had taught them that. For them, work was never a chance to achieve personal growth, but rather simply a way to make a living, a means of paying the bills. That said, slaughtering and processing turkeys for market was not a pleasant way to achieve financial stability. It was a nasty business, assaulting the senses of both smell and sight; the blood of the butchered creatures poured out of the plant into the ditches alongside the street outside.

Ralph got the idea that he might be able to make money raising turkeys instead of slaughtering them; other people were apparently having success at this. This was to prove to be not one of his best ideas. He took a position outside the facility and began driving a truck, delivering the processed birds to their markets.

To put his plan into action, he needed land, and luckily the Mart Posten farm had considerable unused acreage. Even so, there were obstacles from the start. While there was plenty of land, it had no easily accessible source of water, not even a well. Equally problematic was the fact that the house on the land, which was little more than a cabin, was badly in need of rehabilitation. There was no insulation, and it featured the same unpainted wood siding as the Mart Posten house. The tin roof appeared to have shifted in places from the wind catching its edges. And with no well, and initially no electricity, nothing about it suggested easy living.

The cabin was owned by Nettie Wakefield, Ralph's sister who lived in Springfield. Nettie and her family had sometimes used the cottage for weekend visits to her parents. Long after Ralph and Velma moved elsewhere and Mart and Phoebe had died, Ella and Clinton Pruitt had purchased the place. They managed somehow to drag it down the hill to the roadside near the old Mart Posten house. The Pruitts added a room and made it their home for several years.

In the 1970s Johnny Prewett purchased the entire property and built a modern house near the Mart Posten place, which had to be demolished. The cabin remained standing. Decades later, Prewett called members of the Posten family to let them know he was remodeling the cabin to better serve as storage. He had set aside some boards from the original structure and offered them to family members should they want a piece of memorabilia. When the offer was gratefully accepted and family members arrived to see the relics, Prewett pointed out the burned surface of several of the boards, the very pieces of flammable wood that had formed the wall directly behind the wood stove. It appeared the wooden structure had been, at one time, dangerously close to what would have been a devastating fire.

The cabin the Ralph Posten family moved into around 1950 was small, consisting of a living room, a kitchen, and a shed-like addition that served as a bedroom for the entire family, then six in number. The tin roof leaked so badly during rainstorms that Velma had to rush to situate various containers on the floor to catch the streams of water falling from the ceiling. The wood stove in the living room provided little heat for the bedroom, and during the deep chill of winter Velma heated bricks on the wood stove, wrapped them in towels, and placed them at the feet of the sleepers.

The lack of an indoor toilet was something they were used to, and they expected no better. But the absence of a well was another matter. For the first month the cabin had no electricity and was lit by kerosene lamps. To get water, Velma, and often Eddie, had to go down the hill to Mart's place and draw drinking water from the well. A sled pulled by a horse was used to bring up barrels of water from the spring for other household uses and to hydrate the turkeys. When predators were about, Ralph, shotgun at hand, slept on a cot near the gobblers. Meanwhile, he was doing double duty, continuing to drive a truck during the day.

The Posten children walked two miles to the Independence School, where they were taught by Bessie Morrow, the same teacher who had instructed their father. With incredible skill and no additional staff, Bessie was somehow able to teach as well as maintain strict discipline and order—no easy task with all eight grades in one open space.

The dreams of a good financial reward for the turkey venture did not materialize. That hope was crushed when a terrible rainstorm devastated virtually the entire flock. The big birds were out in the open. With no refuge from the falling torrents of water, they ran hopelessly about and drowned by the scores, by the hundreds. In a vain attempt to escape the flood of water, several flew up to the roof of the cabin, where they lay dead and dying. There was a desperate effort to save the afflicted creatures by bringing them into the warmth of the kitchen. The stench of wet, dying poultry permeated the cabin.

Rescue efforts were in vain. The turkey crop was wiped out. Ralph, who was ready to move on, felt well done with both raising turkeys and any other association with those birds that had cost him so much. Thanks to events that were happening in distant parts of the globe and were now reaching the Ozarks, new opportunities were arising. Ralph turned his attention to the construction trade.

The onset of World War II and the creation of Ft. Leonard Wood in the early 1940s opened the way for major construction jobs in the area. The base was a training site for troops as well as a prison for captured German and Italian prisoners of war. There was at least one prison escape: In April of 1944, two German prisoners made their way to freedom. But their freedom was temporary, as they were captured without incident a few days later near the town of Falcon, Missouri.

The building boom that began with the creation of the base was reactivated during the Korean Conflict. Ft. Leonard Wood grew to be a major training center for the military and proved an outstanding economic boost for the region.

The massive enterprise required considerable effort by the army and created pain for many who lived in the area. The U.S.

Army's plan was for an area of 65,000 acres, part of which came from the Mark Twain National Forest. More than 50,000 acres had to be purchased from private landowners.

Although it was sparsely populated, the area did feature several communities, among them Evening Shade, Cookville, Wharton, and Bloodland, the latter of which had been the neighboring community to Benjamin Avery Posten and family.

There was some urgency in getting the huge project going, and the 300 affected families were given deadlines to vacate. While perhaps not important to others, these communities had been there for some time. This was home for the residents. Bloodland not only had several business concerns, but was cherished by the people who lived there. Many of those affected were poor and had lived in the area a long time. Naturally, there was some resistance. In the opinion of most, the army had offered fair prices for the property, but while some people welcomed the chance to sell, others felt lost and grieved at the loss of their home and community. Still others are said to have felt a patriotic pride in yielding their land to a larger cause.[75]

The construction of the fort did wonders for the local economy. Tens of thousands of residents, as well as those who came from a distance, found work there. The population grew significantly in a very short time as workers flocked to the area and real estate prices boomed. For Ralph Posten, it meant the beginning of work in the carpenter trade, better pay, and the honing of skills that would provide for his family for the remainder of his life.

After the turkey disaster there was little reason to remain in the cabin, which had never met the needs of the family. For Velma, the lack of a nearby water supply was a significant handicap to her efforts to care for the family; she was ready to move.

The entire family was eager to leave the cabin, with all its deficiencies and memories of a dream gone bad.

This time they chose a very large two-story house located just a mile from Velma's parents. The house was the very one that Carl's father, Laverne, originally built around the turn of the century.

The ancestral Clark home had been a fine specimen in its day. It featured large rooms, a kitchen, living room, dining room, and a single bedroom downstairs. Three additional bedrooms were upstairs. Porches graced both the front and rear of the house. By the time the Ralph Posten family made it their home in 1952, the luster had worn off and signs of aging were apparent. Again, there was no indoor plumbing or running water, but it was still an upgrade as far as Velma was concerned. She was grateful to have a well just past the back porch. Rent was $25 a month.

Velma especially liked the location, with its proximity to her parents, who lived only a mile away. Just up the road was the farm, pleasingly bordered by a rail fence, of Myrl Clark, her uncle. A short distance down the gravel road in the opposite direction was the site of the Bellefonte School, long gone, but remembered fondly by the Clark children. The move did mean that the children had to change schools from Independence to Fairview, another rural school.

One night in 1953 the children were awoken and told they were going to their grandparents' home for the remainder of the night. Since visiting their grandparents without their parents was unprecedented, this seemed very mysterious, at least to the younger children. But the mystery was solved when their father picked them up the next morning and took them home to meet their new baby brother, David, who had been born that night.

It was during their time at the Clark house that the family was first exposed to television. Previous to actually owning their own black-and-white twenty-one-inch set, they sometimes drove to the nearby farm of Harris and Laura Watson, who welcomed their neighbors to view the Friday night boxing matches. The reception was poor, requiring frequent adjustments, and sometimes someone was sent outside to manually rotate the antenna. The men enjoyed the sporting events though they were of no interest to Velma and the young children. But the technology fascinated everyone. The ability to bring moving pictures, sporting events, situation comedies and nightly news into one's home seemed magical, and the children begged their father to acquire one of these marvels for their own home.

The purchase of the new set was soon made and the outside world came streaming in, which had a great impact on rural families, including the Postens. In some ways the impact was similar to the introduction of the internet decades later. Of course a major difference was that the television did not offer social interaction with others. It did bring in the world, though, in all its black-and-white diversity. In some aspects the Ozarks were still isolated from the world; television provided a new connection and created a new focus in the home, a central gathering place.

Ralph's favorite programs were Westerns. He especially liked the films of John Wayne. *Bonanza* was a weekly treat. The family tuned in to *The Ozark Jubilee*, which was broadcast from Springfield, Missouri, and featured Red Foley and other country singers. They also were entertained by shows starring Slim Pickens Wilson and Chet Atkins. Velma was never very interested in watching television. When she did so, she was often multitasking, doing something constructive with her hands like crocheting or working on a craft project, while at the same time attending to something she was baking in the kitchen.

Despite the lure of television, or perhaps because it did seem so pleasurable, there was a certain restraint about watching it too much, especially during the daytime hours. The rule, mostly unspoken, was that one watched television in the evening after the day's work was done. One neighbor boy revealed that his father would touch the top of the set upon returning from a day at work to see if the device was warm, indicating someone had been watching, breaking the daytime rule, only to try hide that violation by switching it off shortly before their father arrived home.

A HOME OF THEIR OWN

THE MOVE FROM the Clark house in 1954 was a milestone for the Posten family. For the first time they would be homeowners. After years of living in rental houses and dreaming of owning their own, they purchased forty acres from Nettie Wakefield. The land had been part of the Mart Posten farm and lay south of the house where they last lived. Mart died the year before they started to build, and Phoebe was living with other family members.

The house, built on a very tight budget, was put together on weekends and evenings while Ralph continued his full-time job at Ft. Leonard Wood. Members of the construction crew sometimes volunteered their labor on weekends. This was Ralph's first attempt to build a house, and the results demonstrated his lack of experience. The dwelling consisted of an eat-in kitchen, a living room, and three bedrooms. No bathroom; not even a provisional space where one might be added at a later date.

Once again, no indoor plumbing and no running water. A well was required, and Carl Clark arrived to help find the best spot to drill. He went to his task by selecting a forked tree branch. Carrying the limb, he walked slowly around the yard, holding the homemade device about waist high. In theory, when water was detected below the ground the piece of wood would automatically, without any purposeful human action, extend itself downward toward the earth, indicating that water was to be readily found at that location. When Carl was satisfied, he marked the spot for the well to be dug. It did not take the well-digger much time either, as water was discovered at a very low depth.

Sided with stucco, the house was poorly designed. The rooms were not well laid out. One had to go through one bedroom to get to another. There were no hallways. Central heat was once again provided by a wood stove in the living room. In 1960, a long room was added to the rear of the house as a bedroom for all the boys and one of the bedrooms was converted to a bathroom. The family at long last had indoor plumbing, and for the first time, Velma didn't have to go outside to get water for household uses.

The surrounding acreage was part pasture and part timber; a creek ran through it. At the edge of the pasture there were huge piles of stones that Ralph, when yet a child, had picked up and removed from the field. The family used the timber for firewood, which meant using a crosscut saw, as the chainsaw had not yet been introduced into the Posten tool set. The boys had the task of cutting sprouts and bringing in firewood. The wood stove required refills on cold winter nights, and for a time Velma also continued to cook on a wood-fired range.

This was not a farm where a family could earn a living, but elements of farm life continued to be present. Ralph and Velma carefully tended a huge vegetable garden and doled out the duties of hoeing and weed-pulling to the children. A large strawberry patch provided fruit for freezing and for the many batches of strawberry shortcakes that Velma made. The boys went to the small barn to milk a cow or two for the family's dairy needs. Pigs were a common feature, and they were either slaughtered for meat and cooking lard or sold. The slaughtering took place in an open area behind the house, near the barn under a large oak tree. A host of chickens provided eggs and were a frequent offering at Sunday dinners. At times a horse was added to the mix, as were ducks. For a short time the boys took on a goat, but the animal failed to pull a cart as they had hoped and was soon found another home.

Tippy, a Chihuahua mix, was a family pet and sometimes allowed into the house. But most of the dogs were Ralph's blu-etick coonhounds, which were locked in a pen outside and let out only at the time of a hunt, at which time they were wild with excitement to be out on the trail. Ralph prized the dogs for their ability to hunt, but he never personalized them, never formed an attachment. They were for the hunt and not to be regarded as pets.

Once again, and not for the last time, Ralph was drawn back into the Hazelgreen Community where he was born and raised. In the 1950s Hazelgreen was well traveled, as busy Route 66 ran through it. The town had changed significantly since Ralph's youth, but still featured a general merchandise store, a post office, and a Methodist church.

The old Mart Posten house was only a mile north on the gravel road that ran in front of the stucco house. A mile south on the same road brought one to the Gascozark Store, just across a very busy Route 66 from the Gascozark Café, both of which had been built in the 1930s and were situated only a few hundred yards from the Independence Baptist Church. Relatives lived nearby, too. Ralph's sister and brother-in-law,

Augusta and Alfred Reid, had purchased a farm across the road from the stucco house. Ella and Clinton Pruitt, another sister and brother-in-law, and Ralph's brother and sister-in-law, Clyde and Mildred, lived with their family a few miles distant.

Gascozark, like Hazelgreen, was another unincorporated community known as a village or a hamlet. The name was coined by Frank A. Jones, a prominent landowner who built the service station and the café; it combined the names of the Gasconade River and the Ozark region.[76]

Route 66, the famous roadway that led to the creation of Gascozark, was first established in 1926 and grew from a rugged road made of gravel and graded dirt to a fully paved major highway that crossed the United States from Chicago, Illinois, to Santa Monica, California. It was the same road Ralph and Velma took when they made their initial move to California in the late 1930s. Thousands of others took the same route, often in search of a better life.

Decades later, due to increased traffic and ever-larger trucks, the roadway exceeded its capacity to provide safe and efficient travel. The issue of connecting the country with better roads was addressed by President Eisenhower, whose plans to improve the national highway system included replacing the now dangerously narrow and overcrowded Rt. 66. The new highway, built in the mid 1950s, was called I-44.[77]

The years 1954–1964 were busy and eventful years for the Posten family. The children were growing. There were graduations and marriages, and grandchildren started to appear on the scene. Ralph's construction work continued at a steady pace, though there were some brief interruptions. Velma worked at the shoe factory in Richland.

Despite the improved financial state of the family, there

was still not a lot of spare money. Both parents were working, and Velma was doing double duty as factory worker and housekeeper. But Ralph and Velma had lived through the Depression, a profound experience that left its indelible mark. They rarely provided details about those years of scarcity, only hinting at the hardships they'd faced, but sometimes they seemed concerned that it might happen again.

The children were well fed and clothed, but there was a sense that money was in short supply. Perhaps it was for that reason that all of the children sought out part-time jobs after school, on weekends, and during the summer. They picked and sold blackberries, sold Christmas cards door-to-door, worked for area farmers, mowed lawns, and hired out to merchants in Richland. They were never told they must find jobs, but they sought out paid work eagerly and voluntarily, as if it were the natural thing to do. There was a feeling that if they wanted the extras, whether a weekend at the carnival or a special article of clothing, they had better earn the money to make the purchase.

Progress in the form of creature comforts came slowly to the Ozarks. Benjamin Avery homesteaded in the 1870s and obviously did not have electricity or running water, but neither did his son, Mart, eighty years later, and the same was true of their neighbors. Ralph and Velma did not enjoy the convenience of running water or indoor plumbing until the 1960s, and air conditioning came later than that. Once again, the same was true of most of their rural neighbors.

Even if they were slow in arriving, progress and change did come, and as far as Ralph and Velma were concerned, the worst was always behind them. They remembered hard times but did not dwell upon them. They had jobs now, which made all the difference. The availability of jobs and the willingness to earn a livelihood were essentials of the good life, or at least a better one.

Work was considered an aspect of good character. Ralph said he had little use for a man who would not work to support his family. It did not matter what occupation one chose; the mere decision to work at something met his high moral standard. Velma too put a high value on work and would sometimes remark in a letter or conversation upon how members of the family were employed. In 1982 she wrote about her satisfaction that Cora enjoyed her job and that she was glad her grandson, Eddie Posten Jr., was working part-time before heading off to the university. She was pleased too that Eddie's sisters both had good jobs. After saying that, Velma could not resist adding a bit of humor, perhaps a comment that also concealed her own fear: "Seems like everyone has to work anymore. If Reagan takes our social security away, there will be more looking. Ha."

In spite of the value they put on work, people in the rural Ozarks often chose to identify themselves as poor, no matter their financial situation. It was a badge of honor, and one church member repeated the adage, "God must love poor people, he made so many of them." Velma, who often made do with what she had rather than buying a new product, would say, "Poor people have poor ways."

Identifying oneself as "poor" was more an expression of a state of mind than an actual declaration of deprivation. It was a way of saying one was one of the common people, and not privileged, not above anyone else. The same people who declared themselves poor would have objected if some authority had said they were living in poverty. The two terms were not equivalent, and the latter would have seemed a judgment call from an outsider who neither understood nor appreciated their way of life.

Nevertheless, the lack of resources had profound influence on the Postens' lives. Ralph and Velma were born under conditions in which the availability of higher education was either unappreciated or simply out of reach. Both were intelligent and highly capable of learning, but as youths their choices were limited. Velma was pleased to get a high school diploma, but Ralph could eke out only an eighth-grade education before becoming a laborer.

Simply being born and raised in the Ozarks carried a social stigma in the world beyond the hills. One of the best-known labels attached to people of the region is "hillbilly," or "hick" for short. It was used by many as a derogatory term, even if it was sometimes intended to evoke humor. The hick was poor, white, and uneducated, with no culture worth mentioning. They might well live off the grid, probably talked funny, and had no political influence. Their way of speaking, dressing, and interacting with the world was often the subject of ridicule. On the other hand, they were sometimes portrayed as simple people who were out of sync with modern times and short on worldly success, yet filled with practical wisdom. There was the underlying suggestion that maybe they knew best after all, and that the modern world had lost something precious.

As with all stereotypes, these were simplified versions of the truth.

The native Ozarkians more likely simply saw themselves as hardworking, true to their word, plain-speaking, devoted to family and God, and full of common sense. Regardless of the intent of those who called them hillbillies, as often as not no offense was taken. Natives of the region took pride in their past and treasured the lives they lived, and they let others think what they pleased.

Ralph was always alert to what was happening in his rural community. He knew who was ill and who was in the hospital; news traveled fast. Once, Ralph heard a rumor at the Gascozark Store that there had been a shooting in his neighborhood. He brought the news home and he and Velma, troubled and curious and fearing a gunman might be loose in the neighborhood, got in the car and drove back up to the store to learn more about what had happened. The children stayed home behind locked doors.

It was later revealed that the shooter was just fourteen years old. He lived in the area and was visiting a friend who lived directly up the hill from the Posten place. The two had gone into the detached garage, where the visitor had taken a .22-caliber rifle off the shelf, thinking it unloaded, and pointed it at his friend. It accidentally discharged after becoming entangled in his clothing and the bullet struck the victim in the throat, killing him instantly. Stunned by the death of his friend, the fourteen-year-old ran from the scene. The incident was determined to be an accident, but some local people maintained suspicions to the contrary.

Saturday was the day to go shopping. Ralph and Velma, along with the younger children, drove to Richland and parked near the H.E. Warren & Sons store, which featured both a grocery and a department store, and later a dime store. While Velma did the grocery shopping, Ralph picked up an item from the hardware, went over for a haircut at Dick's Barber Shop, or simply found neighbors to chat with. On Saturdays everyone went to town; people drove from miles around to do their marketing and enjoy an active informal social day.

The seven-mile drive to Richland on Saturday mornings was sometimes briefly halted. The car would come to a slow crawl on the narrow, winding road as it approached a wagon pulled by two horses. In the driver's seat was neighbor Cleve Carroll, who never considered it necessary to transition to the automobile. His wife, Emma, sat beside him wrapped in clothing sufficient to ward out the cold or keep out the sun, according to the dictates of the weather. Once in town Cleve parked the team at the blacksmith shop and Emma shopped for groceries.

Neither work nor weather stopped Ralph from finding time to enjoy the sports that were his trademarks: fishing and hunting. He was never happier than when he was doing either, planning to do so, or recapping the event afterwards. He either set trotlines or took the boat out at night, rigged with a light, to gig for fish according to the season. No fishing pole or rod and reel for him. After the trotline was set and the appropriate bait was attached, he took the boat to shore and temporarily left the area to do other chores. The line was then checked at intervals. Usually that meant returning to the scene very early in the morning, when the river was often wrapped in cloudlike vapor.

Ralph's hunting interests were many. He hunted squirrels, rabbits, turkeys, and deer according to season, all of which became bounty for the dinner table. He loved to let out the dogs at night and go into the woods in hopes of catching the trail of a raccoon or opossum, although the names were always shortened to "coon" and "possum." The thrill was not so much in capturing or killing the hunted creatures; often they were not harmed at all. The excitement lay in listening for the dogs to pick up a trail and follow it to its source, where they would bark vigorously and triumphantly as the seasoned hunter, aware of which dog was barking first, made his way to join them at the site of their conquest. But there were also some years when the hides of raccoons were highly prized, and Ralph obliged, selling hides to the vendor.

Ralph's hunting and fishing skills were valued. His knowledge of the best places and times to go, his reputation for being good company, and his enthusiasm for the sport made others seek him out as a guide or companion. He was delighted when his eldest son, Eddie, and later some of his grandchildren, including Jeff, Jerry, and Mike Hake, shared his interests. In late life he regretted failing to take the men of the family on a hunting trip to Canada, a trip he had long considered.

The man was as intent about his sport as he was about his work. A high-energy person, he often went full throttle. He had little patience for sluggards and for those who did not put forward their best effort. Despite enjoying the hunt as a social occasion, he was not interested in teaching others how to hunt or properly use firearms. He expected his companions to have already acquired those basic skills, and if not, to do nothing to obstruct him from his own path. He simply loved the outdoors and in many ways called forth the frontier traditions of his grandfather, who died more than ten years before his birth. The two had much in common: a love of the outdoors and of fishing and hunting, a deeply religious life, and a rural life with the family at its center.

Ralph had no desire for city life. The rural domain was his beloved home. Even when he was not employed in sport, whenever he was in the woods he was looking for signs of game, observing the geese in flight, joining the family to pick up walnuts to be dried, hulled, and shelled for the goodies inside. He liked to go down to the river bottom in search of the pa pa trees that grew on the riverbanks and bore the fruit known as the bananas of his youth.

Ralph stood five foot seven inches tall and weighed most of his adult life less than one hundred and forty-five pounds, but he was muscular from a life of labor and general physical activity. He had great energy and was capable of working all day on construction, coming home, cleaning up for supper, resting briefly, and then going out for a nighttime hunting or fishing expedition. When he worked, he worked hard, whether the task was building a house or cutting firewood. When he played, he played just as hard.

Extremely cold weather was painful for Ralph's arthritic hands, though, and he did not enjoy working out of doors in frigid weather, as a construction project sometimes required. But he was resolute in doing what he had to do, so he would bundle up carefully, grab his lunchbox complete with a Twinkie (his favorite), and head out to the job without complaint, and in some cases with a word of humor about his predicament.

A man of strong faith and with deep connections to his church, Ralph was nevertheless at ease with the coarse language used by men on the construction crews. When he chose to include some of that language in his own speech, it was done only in certain places and only in the presence of men. The notion of protecting women from foul language was common. Ralph's brother, Lewis, was known to demand a visitor apologize for using an objectionable word in his wife's presence.

Ralph had strong emotions but kept them contained, for the most part. He was prone to biting his lower lip and walking silently away from a scene that was arousing his distress. This occurred once in a church business meeting during a discussion about purchasing new pews. There was much disagreement, some wanting one style and some another, some favoring a lighter color over a darker color, etc. Something in the process of the discussion angered Ralph. It was not a matter of failing to get approval for his preferences, whatever they may have been, but the manner in which the arguments were being carried out that angered him. Biting his lower lip, he walked away from the debate. He was not known to shed tears easily and did so rarely. One exception was the morning after the death of his father. That morning, deeply grieving over the loss, he stood in the kitchen, reached down and picked up his infant son, David, who was less than a year old, held him in his arms and wept.

The Posten family did not typically take vacations, but they did sometimes take day-long excursions. In some years, construction work was seasonal, and Ralph worked on projects around the acreage or went fishing or hunting. The one-day holidays often consisted of going to either a gravel bar on the Gasconade where the kids could swim and have a picnic lunch, or to another convenient outdoor spot. During one of their longer excursions, the family drove to the Branson area, a sleepy little town in a beautiful, picturesque rural setting that had not yet become a country music haven. One of the points of interest was the Shepherd of the Hills site, which paid homage to the characters created by Harold Bell Wright in his novel by the same name. Ralph had been working on a construction crew building a bridge on the White River, so he was familiar with the area. As part of the adventure the family boarded a barge for a trip down the White River, but the day rapidly turned stormy. The wind came up, the water was turbulent. The anticipated scenic joyride turned out to be a treacherous one. The strong current and wind were moving the boat this way and that; the tugboat could barely maintain its course and the barge was nearly out of control. Fear was plainly printed on the faces of all the passengers as the boat threatened to crash into one of the piers on the new bridge. Anxiety turned to relief as the boat was at last brought under control and the barge safely reached land.

THE RELIGIOUS LIFE

THE IMPORTANCE OF a Christian life, as defined by the faith and doctrine of the local church, was greatly emphasized in the Posten family and affected all aspects of life. Independence Baptist Church had been the center of much of their spiritual and social lives since its start in the 1920s, when Mart and Phoebe Posten were charter members.

Over the years, many members of the extended family attended, but Ralph was not an active member until he was nearly thirty. One day at the supper table while the family was still living in the cabin and working the turkey farm, he simply announced that henceforth, meals would be preceded by saying grace and churchgoing on a regular basis was soon to follow. He eventually assumed a leadership role in the church as a teacher, superintendent, liberal financial contributor, and deacon.

Church attendance came to be a thrice-weekly occurrence. Sunday morning featured Sunday school and worship service. Sunday evening was time for Training Union and another worship service. Wednesday evenings were reserved for prayer meeting. Ralph faithfully attended all three services.

Velma was more likely to remain home on Wednesday evenings and sometimes did not attend Sunday evenings either.

Although she was a participant in church life and taught a youth Sunday school class, she had less interest in specifically Baptist traditions and beliefs, and put more emphasis on the general tenets of living a Christian life.

The Clark family, while also Baptists, tended to view religion in broad general terms; a softer version of Christianity. They held that one should go to church on Sunday morning and try to live a moral life following the traditional values of right and wrong, but there was no emphasis on reading or quoting the Bible, nor did they speak of religious matters in social settings. They would have fared just as well in association with a Methodist, Presbyterian, or some other Protestant congregation.

In marked contrast, the Posten brand adhered to the Bible as the literal word of God, and they were content only with a religious practice that followed that standard. They studied, discussed, and at times debated the meanings of Biblical passages.

There were two revivals a year, typically in the spring and fall, led by an evangelist who spoke every night for one to two weeks. The protracted meetings of years past had long gone by the wayside, but the goals of the meetings—salvation through Christ, and for believers to renew their commitments—remained the same. Every meeting was certain to detail the horrors of hell and the bliss of heaven. At the conclusion of every service there was an altar call during which troubled souls were invited to make the choice and come forward to experience the "new birth."

This was all in perfect harmony with the teachings of Baptist ministers throughout the community, who saw their primary mission as enabling others to avoid the terror of hell and enjoy the assurance of heaven. Many of the traditions and rituals were much the same as they were in Benjamin Avery's day.

There were excellent orators among the ministers and evangelists, some of whom who could skillfully illustrate their subject matter in the most vivid—whether blissful or draconian—terms, depending upon the ultimate eternal destination they were describing. Virgil Manes, a minister with a long, dedicated ministry at both Independence Baptist Church as well as several other churches in the area, was exceptional in this regard. Not only was he skilled in structuring his message to fit the audience so that it could be clearly understood, but he punctuated it with real-life illustrations that made the sermon come alive. His was an emotional delivery as well. When Reverend Manes described the horrors of hell and the everlasting torture it entailed, his face turned red. You knew he not only meant what he was saying but he felt it deep in his heart, and no one listening wanted to go to the lake of eternal fire where people were crying out for just a simple drink of water. Given the two choices, most people worried about such a fate and opted for the better choice.

The flipside to eternal damnation got good coverage, too. The beauty and eternal restfulness of heaven, the glory of being with God and reuniting with deceased family members was a theme clearly presented and well received. As one older parishioner once said, remembering some of these great speakers, "When one of those preachers preached a funeral, the glories of heaven sounded so wonderful that you almost wished you could trade places with the deceased."

Despite the gravity of their messages, the preachers were also capable of humor. The sign of a good speaker was knowing just when and what kind of humor to use. One might go for the long story with a comical twist. Others went for the short punchline. For some, humor was subtle, as it was with Reverend

Manes. After one Sunday service he approached Bonnie Adams and Mary Ann Southern, Ralph's nieces, after the service and asked about their husbands, who were noticeably absent. When they hesitated he guessed the truth: that their spouses had gone hunting for the day. He smiled, unoffended, and said, "I get up there and preach the gospel and those men take their guns and are ready to go out there and defend it."

Periodically, baptisms were performed for the newly converted. The watery event was done in the Gasconade River by total immersion, just as it had been done for generations. The Independence Baptist Church's favorite spot to perform this ritual was just below what was then called the low-water bridge, a couple miles from the church.

Ralph was a fundamentalist. He believed wholeheartedly that the Bible was the literal word of God, a belief consistent with his religious heritage. For Ralph there was right and wrong, and not much room for something in between. His siblings, all of whom were of the same faith, sometimes joined in on discussions of a Biblical topic at family gatherings.

One topic that got little agreement, whether among the local ministers or members of the congregations, was the second coming of Jesus Christ. All believed the climactic would occur—that Jesus would literally come back to earth and that the faithful could anticipate that day happening very soon. It was the details that caused confusion and disagreement. The book of Revelation was difficult to decipher. The topics of the thousand-year reign, the rising of the dead from their graves, the ascension into heaven, and what happened to those left behind were all subjects where the meanings were parsed without conclusive answers that satisfied everyone. The ministers were able to weed through the confusion somewhat by being adamant about the main point: the apocalyptic event would happen, and given the state of the world, it would probably be sooner than later. Get ready now, was the urgent call.

Ralph's beliefs were solid and often unyielding, but he was also prayerful, earnest in his desire to understand more, and humble in his own place among men. He did not believe that being a Christian made him better or less than anyone else. All were equally sinners and in need of the grace of God. He also gave voice to the social aspects of the Christian message, believing it was an act of faith to give to the less fortunate, help the orphans and the poor. An ardent teetotaler who abandoned alcohol after his youth, he would not hesitate to stop the car, much to Velma's chagrin, and give a ride to the man known as the town drunk, whose odoriferous aroma gave witness to his reputation as he entered the car.

Ralph was also respected and trusted, and he was concerned about the welfare of his community. He was often the first call for other residents when there was a life-changing event: a suicide, a fire, an accident, an illness. He spent many nights in bedside vigil for those who were dying. Sitting with the very ill, with those near death, was a tradition about which little was spoken. It was simply understood that those teetering on that narrow edge between life and death needed someone as witness, a silent comforter. That was the job, just to sit in silence. Perhaps the sitter, if he were so inclined, would offer a silent prayer or share a few words, all in a deeply felt sense of shared humanity.

One issue that tested Ralph's beliefs and traditions was Roman Catholicism, which was regarded with critical suspicion not only by his own faith community but also by other Protestant churches throughout the country.

This concern became most prominent during the candidacy of John F. Kennedy for president. Protestants, perhaps still retaining ancient memories of the persecution of their ancestors in Europe, were deeply committed to separation of church and state and feared a Catholic president might be unduly influenced by the papacy. So great was the problem for Kennedy that he found it necessary to make a televised speech declaring in no uncertain terms that his decisions as president would be free of interference from any church official and that he would honor separation of church and state.

In the rural Ozarks, which were largely Protestant, the Catholic church was believed to deny members direct access to Christ, requiring a priest to act as middle-man. Congregants likely were not versed in the doctrines of that faith or may not even have known personally one of its adherents, but the bias was there and was openly declared from the pulpit. Upon hearing about the planned marriage of one of his young congregants to a Catholic, one Baptist minister was observed to sadly shake his head and remark, "Looks like we lost another one."

This was the context in which Ralph found himself upon learning the plans of his only and beloved daughter to marry a man of that faith. There was no one to whom he might have gone for wise and unbiased counsel on this matter, had he sought to do so. He had to weigh the issue carefully by himself, which he did, giving the matter reflection and prayer. He made no overt protest. Instead he went quietly along, pleased to attend his daughter's wedding, even if uncomfortable in a Catholic Church for the first time. It was not long before his reservations softened even more and in time all but disappeared as he found his new son-in-law to be a faithful husband, a good provider, and earnest in his own faith.

Ralph's attitude about race, while affected by several factors, was in part impacted by his religion. The Southern Baptist Convention, of which his church was a member, had been created in 1845 over the very issue of slavery, which they supported, a problem that affected other Protestant groups as well. Long after slavery was no longer the disputed point, the country's perception of race was being tested and modified. Some ideas changed, some did not. The lingering effect of those prejudices prompted the Southern Baptist Convention in 1995 to officially apologize for its past support of racism.

Even in 1940 there were very few African Americans living in the rural Ozarks. Regional attitudes reflected those prevalent throughout the South. The creation of Ft. Leonard Wood eventually helped increase racial diversity in the area, but in its beginning it was plagued with issues as it dealt with national and local prejudices.

The subject of racial equality was brought to Ralph's attention during the 1960s, a period of national unrest with a dedicated push for civil rights. The media coverage of marches, sometimes fiery speeches by African American leaders, and confrontations with the police tended to reinforce existing stereotypes.

Typical of Ralph's mode of thinking, he viewed the issue of equal rights and access in the context of his own church. An angry group of marchers demanding membership in an all-white church was an unlikely scenario in the rural Ozarks, but the concept did feed into his thinking. He would welcome African Americans into church membership, but only if they came as sincere individuals truly wanting to worship in harmony with the beliefs and practices of that congregation.

True to his word, years later when a retired military couple of mixed race purchased a home hear Ralph and Velma, they were not only invited to church but also into the Postens' home. Even then, Velma's one concern had nothing to do with color, but that the couple, who had been previously stationed in Japan, had picked up the custom of removing their shoes upon entering a house. Velma was not prepared to strip to her bare feet.

The church was not only the spiritual home for the Posten family, but also the primary center of their social life. There was often a potluck dinner after church on Sunday, and the annual all-ages Halloween party was well attended. Such events were held in the church basement. The church also hosted hayrides, trips to the skating rink in Lebanon, and on rare occasion, an individual teacher might sponsor a small group to attend a theater showing a Bible-themed film.

It was common to have guests, including the minister or other church members, for Sunday dinner, which was the biggest and best of the week. Velma worked throughout Saturday afternoon and early Sunday morning to prepare as much in advance as possible and have a hot meal on the table shortly after returning from church services. A cake or homemade pie was often included as a special dessert.

The other primary source for their social life was family. There were many relatives nearby, especially on Ralph's side of the family. Five of his sisters—Ella, Ada, Lilly, Augusta, and Nettie—as well as his brother Clyde all lived within reasonable driving distance. Ralph had a clear preference for being with his own relatives, his siblings and other extended members of the Posten family. Velma had far less contact with her side of the family, and not being able to drive kept her from making independent visits. Relatives from California and Oklahoma made yearly visits. The children were always most interested in visits from those who had children with whom they could play.

Sunday afternoon was a time for visiting, either receiving guests in their home or going out themselves. In either case this was all done by invitation. Someone simply dropped by, stayed for a time, then went on their way. There were also special celebrations. February 14, 1960, fell on a cold but sunny winter day. After church, several relatives, friends, and the minister went to Ella and Clinton Pruitt's home to greet Phoebe Posten and celebrate her birthday.

Sunday was considered a day of rest. Any commercial activity was not only frowned upon but also legally restricted under local blue laws. In the rural Ozarks there were few public distractions on Sunday, as all nonessential businesses were closed.

Working on Sunday was also discouraged. Ralph avoided labor on that day, yet it was not uncommon for him to get restless and pick up his rifle on a lazy, cloudy afternoon and declare he was going for a walk in the woods to see if he could see a squirrel. Despite the no-work rule, Velma was still in the kitchen getting Sunday dinner together, and the minister was hard at work delivering his morning and evening sermons. And there were few objections when Rush Johnson, owner of the Gascozark Store, opened it briefly after church for the convenience of church members.

In the summer, making ice cream was a special treat. Ralph would purchase a block of ice, place it in a gunny sack, crush it, then place it one portion at a time into the freezer, applying salt and more ice as needed. Velma had already readied the mix. Those were the days of hand cranks, and various participants took turns applying muscle until the ice cream got thick and the handle was difficult to turn. Meanwhile, Velma made chocolate frosting, a perennial favorite of the children.

Large holiday gatherings followed a traditional pattern,

with the men in one room talking of guns, cars, and work while columns of smoke filled the room, sucking the oxygen out of the air, the men either unaware or unconcerned about the long-term health consequences yet to follow. In fair weather the men sometimes got out their guns and wandered into the woods, suggesting they were in a casual hunting mode, conversing as they strolled along the edge of the forest. Not a serious hunt, as no game was actually acquired, but rather a unifying ritual of brotherhood, as the men had no tradition of men simply taking a walk together.

In the kitchen and dining room the women were busy preparing the meal or cleaning up afterwards. Still, their laughter and sometimes hushed conversation were an assurance that they too were having a good time despite the extra duties their role gave them. The children played outside or hovered around the edges of the rooms, gleaning what they could from the adult conversations.

Ella and Clinton Pruitt were occasional evening visitors who came over for a game of rook, a card game at which Ralph excelled and in which Velma participated just to complete the number of required players.

Humor was present in all such gatherings, as Ralph and his siblings loved to laugh. Even the relating of ordinary incidents could bring about the desired lighthearted response if told right. Velma too had a sense of humor and an appreciation of laughter, which reached its pinnacle when she had occasion to get together with her sister, Verga. Their shared humor was often intimate, intense, and seemed to possess each of them. At times their hushed tones made one suspect that something of a secret, even risqué, nature was being shared.

The couple had different viewpoints about having guests.

Ralph, on one hand, loved visitors at any time. Relatives, friends, people he had just met, strangers—it made no difference. He loved to talk, did so easily with anyone, and welcomed all. After church on Sunday, while Velma and the children waited in the car, eager to go home, he could be found standing on the church steps in conversation. Velma, on the other hand, was a more private person. She preferred visitors to be family or close friends, and when they dropped by just anytime, especially around dinner, she was concerned. Throughout her life she enjoyed visits from her adult children, and later, her grandchildren, at various times hosting them in her home for several days.

Velma was intensely loyal to her family, hardworking, and creative in her approach to the many tasks she faced. The lack of extra money to purchase items needed for a school project was solved as Velma would take whatever materials were at hand and create something to fill the need. At times she made dresses for her daughter and shirts for the boys. She was also opinionated and could be quite critical, not reluctant to tell her children how she felt about an action they had taken. She was also devoted, protective, and would defend family members against any criticism from others.

There were often afterschool homemade treats for the children. She sometimes read traditional children's stories such as the *Three Bears*. Velma was skilled in the use of little songs to mock the antics of self-indulgent children. One of her favorites was "Nobody loves me. Everybody hates me. I am just going to eat some juicy worms." She had other ways of dealing with the children when they were whining for something they did not need. On the way home from church on a hot humid Sunday night the kids might beg their parents to stop for ice cream or soda pop, but Velma would challenge the cries with cool deliberation: "Oh, let's just wait until we get home and drink a cold glass of water."

She loved flowers and had numerous houseplants, all of which flourished under her care. She was fond of crochet and needlework and enjoyed numerous other crafts. A doll collection displayed in the dining room grew over time as family members added to the cache.

The minister who conducted her funeral but never knew her personally heaped honors on her for being an old-fashioned mother who stayed at home and took care of the kids, but that stereotype did not perfectly fit. She was more than that. She was a full-time homemaker, which was even more difficult in those months when Ralph's construction work took him away from home for an entire week and left her with all the child care as well as all the duties around the home. There were chores to be done, cows to be milked, dogs to be looked after, and firewood to be brought in. The children helped, but Velma was in charge. And she was doing all this while working outside the home, spending years at the shoe factory and later at the H.D. Lee garment factory, both in Richland.

Taking a job outside the home was a lot of extra work, but Velma was pleased to be able to help provide financially for the family, and she appreciated the chance to get outside the house, away from the children and her spouse, and simply mingle with other women. This was one way she created her own space, a place where she could have friends apart from the domestic scene.

The couple did follow traditional roles. Ralph attended to the maintenance of the house and farm and anything having to do with the car. Velma was responsible for all the household chores, including cooking. Her spouse was content to provide neither help nor interference in that department, and left the kitchen entirely to her domain. On the rare times Velma was away, as when she traveled to California to visit Verga, he did not so much as make a cup of coffee. Entering the kitchen was like traversing a foreign land. In the absence of his wife, he preferred to go to the Oasis Truck Stop, where he could enjoy not only coffee and food, but conversation as well.

Following traditional roles did not necessarily mean that everything was evenly balanced. Ralph loved the children, provided for them, and treated them well; in later life he said one of the happiest times of his life was when the children were young. Even so, the role he played in the family provided him much more freedom than Velma was allowed. After both had been working at their individual jobs all day, Ralph felt free to leave the house and children completely in the care of his wife while he pursued whatever fishing or hunting adventure was available at that time. He enjoyed many sporting holidays throughout the year, days when he simply took off in pursuit of his recreation. He could, and did, leave easily. She could not, and did not, even had she wanted to do so.

GOING INDEPENDENT

In the early 1960s Ralph made a big decision; he would stop working as a carpenter for others and strike out on his own. He was already in his mid forties and such a decision took considerable courage. He saw the possibilities of making a good living building houses on his own and he wanted to be his own boss for a change. At this stage in his work life he felt confident that he could do so. To that end he sold the stucco house and purchased a lot in Richland, perhaps to provide a more visible location for the business he was starting. The move also benefited Velma, as the factory where she worked was a short distance from the site of the new house. Now she could easily walk to work. Whatever the reasons may have been for the move, they were quite persuasive, for Ralph was not a person who enjoyed living in a city, even if that city had a population of less than two thousand souls.

The backyard of the new house bordered the railroad track, an intrusion which was easily accommodated. Moving to town meant not only selling the house and forty acres in Hazelgreen, but also leaving the Laquey School District, where Ralph had been elected a member of the school board. Ralph was ready to leave both concerns and move in a different direction.

At the time Ralph started his business, FHA loans had become readily available to individuals with modest incomes who could make a small down payment. Working people in the area could afford to build a new home, and they were among Ralph's first customers. One Richland resident who lived in one of those houses for over thirty years commented, "Ralph did not make fancy houses, but he made good houses." In time Ralph attracted more affluent customers and the business took on repair projects as well, including work on the historic Civil War home of Calloway Manes.

The business soon grew and prospered. The growth was due in part to an improving economy and the availability of government loans. Of equal importance was the fact that Ralph was a good carpenter who happened to build affordable homes. His reputation as a trustworthy man of good character, well regarded in the community, was also essential to his business success. But Ralph was not an ambitious man, at least not in a business sense. His connections to the community provided many opportunities for investment and expansion, but he had no interest in building an empire. He wanted to make a good living for himself and his crew and still have time to relax, support his church, and do the sporting activities he so enjoyed.

Whatever expertise he achieved as a businessman he learned on the job, making mistakes along the way, for he had no business background. He was sometimes frustrated by his lack of formal education. David, who joined his father in the building business after graduation from high school, recalled that in the beginning Ralph had no formal housing plans and created loosely conceived contracts with customers, sometimes sketching out a house design on the back of an envelope, giving an estimate of the cost, and shaking hands in agreement.

As the business grew, so did the crew, which in addition to the two full-time carpenters included David and sometimes Carl and Eddie.

In 1964 Ralph won a new Chevrolet in a drawing at the Shriners' Circus sponsored by the Lions Club. Soon after, he, Velma, and David drove to California to visit relatives. The vehicle had no air conditioning and the trip was fast-paced. Ralph wanted to reach the destination as soon as possible and had little interest in stopping for roadside attractions. For David, it seemed the entire trip took only seven days.

A few years later, Ralph purchased forty acres just outside the city limits of Richland. He tore down the existing house, believing it was better to start from scratch than to rehabilitate an old house, and built a modern brick ranch house in its place. The move was paralleled by Velma's retirement from employment outside the home, but she remained quite busy, especially since Ralph typically had his entire crew for lunch in his home. This was no quick eat-and-run affair, either. Velma prepared large meals with all the trimmings. No crew ever had it better at lunchtime.

In time, a horse and a few calves were added to the little farm. Elements of farm life would follow the Postens always. Soon, Carl Clark came to live with Ralph and Velma. He remained there until his health deteriorated and Velma could no longer care for him, at which time he was moved to a nursing home in Lebanon.

RETIREMENT

THE DECISION TO move yet again came about due to a combination of circumstances. The success of the business meant that Ralph's life had become more stressful. That was the less-desirable aspect of being independently employed. The life of a contractor did not stop with a five o'clock whistle, and customers continued to make requests, lodge complaints, and call about other matters long after the traditional quitting time. In addition, the cost of lumber and other building supplies fluctuated, making it difficult to adequately predict costs and thereby make a reasonable profit. The prospect of retirement was sounding more and more attractive, and Ralph was formulating a plan. He dreamed of being debt free and living again closer to fishing and hunting opportunities in the Hazelgreen community.

The plan went as imagined. The sale of the home and acreage did generate enough profit to pay off the mortgage, build a new home, and purchase a new truck, as well as provide extra savings. Velma had loved the house and was known to have said that home was the only one she had sadness about leaving. Even her modest reluctance was unusual, for whatever her interests may have been throughout the years, she had always been willing to move where and when her husband desired. She saw herself in a supportive role willing to follow her husband's lead in such matters. She very soon loved her new home, thankfully, and valued the status of being debt free.

The building site for the new home was a lot that had been part of a large farm. The owner had decided to sell a few lots for the construction of individual homes, and the purchase by the Postens was the first. The property was served by Highway 133, the primary connection between Richland and I-44. Later when the road was revamped, the main roadway, 133, was moved farther east and that portion of the old road became known as Utica Drive.

Back in Hazelgreen, they were in familiar territory. Both the old Mart Posten place as well as the first house Ralph and Velma owned were only a mile distant. To the west, down the bluff, across the slough, over the field, and beyond the river was the farm where they had been tenants nearly a half century earlier. The old tenant house, its roof damaged and the chimney crumbling, was now a storage shed for hay, and was visible from the top of the bluff. The Independence Baptist Church was only a mile away as well. Home again.

Hazelgreen was Ralph's primary community, and it was still flourishing in his youth. Even prior to his birth in 1916 the little village featured a number of business establishments including a bank, a barber shop, and a picture gallery. The school, a log structure dating from the time of the Civil War, stood until 1948. In the town's prime there was a popular and well-attended annual picnic, and a lodge for travelers. Parson's Grocery was open into the 1950s, at which time the new highway cut through the community, leaving only a few homes, the

Methodist church, and the Hazelgreen Cemetery, the final resting place for many from both the Posten and Clark families.

Once he and Velma were settled at the new property, Ralph purchased an additional seven acres, a forested piece of land that lay directly across the road from his home. Much of that acreage was on a steep grade, unsuitable for building or much else. But it suited the fisherman, whose goal was access to the river. The feature that interested him was the old dirt and gravel road that snaked its way down the hill and across the slough. Ralph was on good terms with the farmer who owned the bottomland, which was rarely planted due to annual flooding, and he got permission to walk across it and reach the river directly from his home. There was neither a dock nor a place for one, so Ralph improvised by securing his boat to the trunk of a tree that stood at the water's edge. Now he also had transportation for river excursions.

Years later, in September of 1988, he sold the seven acres to Don. "Easy terms," Ralph had said as he made the deal, tacking on six percent interest to the contract. The installments were to be paid in small amounts and administered by the Pulaski County Bank. There was calculation in all this. He had been living with cancer and correctly understood that his time was short. Selling the land to his son was a good way to keep the property in the family and yet provide a small supplemental income for Velma once he was gone. It is likely he also felt it a good fiscal experience for his son. He died the following year.

In the late 1970s, Lewis and Cora Posten announced they were soon retiring and wanted move back to Missouri from California, where they had lived and worked most of their adult lives. Ralph helped secure a lot adjacent to his own home and made arrangements with the couple to build a home very similar to the one he had built for himself and Velma.

In May of 1977, Lewis, still in California, wrote noting some details to be added to the house, which was in the process of being built. First there were the considerations about his health. "I hope you are ok. We are pretty good now. Cora still doesn't walk too good. I have trouble getting the old zip back after that surgery. Mostly of what bothers me is the stomach. That's my weakest place I guess." He wrote that he was uncertain about the exact date he would retire but that it would be soon. He went on to list his concerns about the house. Had the deed been changed over? Yes, they did want a built-in dishwasher and carpet in the living room. "This is the first time we have helped you build a house. So you can straighten out what we don't see." He and Cora were looking forward to the relocation. "I am sure we will enjoy living there again. I am sure going to fish and hunt some and work a little. We are planning on lots of good times, the four of us. Some before you retire and a lot after."

The new house was completed. Lewis retired and he and Cora moved back to the Ozarks, next door to their siblings. For various reasons, the anticipated companionship envisioned by Lewis in his letter never developed in the way he imagined. As individuals and couples they each had their own way of doing things. Although the relationships were cordial, they never achieved the degree of intimacy one might have predicted and which the participants expected.

Rather than doing an activity together, they often went their separate ways, even though it might have seemed easy and natural to do it together. For example, Ralph and Lewis both liked to fish and hunt, but each man had his own firm ideas about how to go about those pursuits, so they did not enjoy sharing that important recreation. Ralph also was far more gregarious, having spent years sharing his sporting events with other men, while Lewis tended to value his time alone more.

Even after the deaths of their husbands, Lewis in 1985 and Ralph in 1989, the relationship between the two sisters, while outwardly friendly, did not flourish. One indication of their separation had to do with transportation. Cora drove; Velma did not, and was reluctant to ask Cora, who was not generous with offers. They each lived in comfortable homes, side by side, while maintaining very separate domains.

Early retirement at sixty-two was a good choice for Ralph. As planned, he had time for his favorite pastime, and he continued to work closely with his church. Velma put more energy into a garden club, the Hilltoppers. In December of 1882 she wrote an article for the *Richland Mirror* describing the recent activities of the club, which included an all-day meeting where they made gifts for nursing home residents. Velma also continued to enjoy working with flowers and houseplants, helped with the garden, and applied her hand to a number of crafts. The couple enjoyed visits from the family, especially the grandchildren. Ralph and Velma both took pride in their vegetable garden, which grew much more produce than the two could use; the excess was given to family and neighbors. They spent more time together, going to auctions, gospel sings, and to visit relatives.

At times, after retirement, Ralph worked on short-term assignments for David, who had taken over the building business. In 1985 Ralph temporarily supervised some remodeling for public housing in Richland. That job was not well paid, but as Velma said, "It will help out." Despite their reduced income, with reliance on social security and modest savings, retirement met their expectations and did not limit them from anything they wanted to do. They had not had visions of exotic cruises or other expensive enterprises requiring deep pockets, and would not have pursued those activities even had they unlimited means to do so. Rather, they were content with the usual pattern of their lives, felt fortunate to have a comfortable home without a mortgage, to be debt free and in health good enough to continue life as usual with their extended family, their church, and members of their rural community.

A GRIM DIAGNOSIS

FAR TOO SOON the days of contented retirement came to end when Ralph was diagnosed with lung cancer. When Clyde, his younger brother, died from that disease in 1975, Ralph, previously a heavy smoker, stopped cold turkey. Just not soon enough. The damage had been done.

He had experienced other health problems as well. The most serious had been bleeding ulcers, several years before the cancer diagnosis. At that time he was hospitalized in Lebanon, Missouri, but he did not respond well to treatment and his condition was complicated when he acquired an infection. After nearly a month in the hospital with no sign of improvement and his health actually diminishing, Velma called in another doctor for a second opinion. That doctor questioned the treatment Ralph was receiving and had him transferred to a hospital in Springfield, where recovery finally began. In 1968 Ralph was briefly hospitalized with pneumonia.

Ralph was around seventy years of age at the time of the cancer diagnosis, and the doctors advised him there would be no recovery. The tumor was inoperable. The best they could do was to start radiation, shrink the tumor, and hope to prolong his life. At his request for more information, the doctors suggested that he might have as long as twenty-two months to live, perhaps less.

The family was familiar with cancer. In addition to Ralph's brother, his sister Ada had died of the disease. Velma had lost both a niece and a nephew to it. Concerned about their own livelihood, the couple had years earlier purchased an insurance policy specific to that infirmity. Unfortunately, when help was needed, the plan paid practically nothing. Medicare paid for the bulk of Ralph's medical treatment.

For many months Ralph lived with the knowledge that his life had a more definitive timeline than before. He certainly had always known he would someday die and he had thought about his own mortality, but now what had been generalized had become specific. He had said that he felt it was important for the old to die to make room for the younger generation. He had also philosophized that it was ironic that just when one reached an age where he had learned some important lessons about life and how to live it, it was time for him to die. Now it was his turn, and like any thoughtful person, he grappled with the meaning of it all. At times he felt better physically, other times worse. There may even have been moments when lack of pain and extra energy gave him reason to believe he might survive after all. Fortunately, there were medications to help keep the worst of the pain at bay.

The medications created an incident of interest in the household. Visitors would stop by briefly, knowing Ralph was seriously ill. One visitor came several times to express her concern, and on more than one occasion asked to use the restroom, which happened to be the place where the medications were kept. After a few of these occurrences, Velma noted that pills were disappearing far too rapidly. She knew the sick man had not been taking that many. Something seemed amiss, but she could not be certain. To test her theory she created a sign which read simply, "Keep away from the medications. This means you," and placed it in a prominent position near the drugs. When the suspect paid another visit and used the restroom as usual, she apparently took the message to heart. She made a quick exit and did not come again. The mystery was solved.

Radiation did at first shrink the tumor, and Ralph was driven many times to Springfield for treatments. On the return home from one such trip in September of 1988, he seemed emotional, and wanted to talk as he lay in the back seat of the car. "From what I have picked up," he said, "unless the Lord intervenes, I have about a year to live." After a moment of silence he changed the subject slightly to talk about the spouse he would leave behind. "I think she ought to sell the place and rent in town. She's always liked to travel. I never have. I think she ought to enjoy the money." Growing increasingly emotional, now tearful, he concluded, "It's hard to talk about dying, but it's good to talk about it."

During the last year of his life Ralph had increased fatigue and loss of strength, even once admitting, "I'm just losing it." Nevertheless, he continued to make efforts to keep active, although he was often not feeling well. Only a few months before his death, with no particular goal in mind other than to get out of the house for a time, he took his gun, got in the truck, and drove toward the nearby community of Brownfield. As he approached the Gascozark Resort he saw that a tractor had somehow slid into a ditch and the driver could not get it out of the mud. Although Ralph was in pain, he stopped the truck, got out, secured a chain to the stranded vehicle, and pulled it onto the road. Ralph did not easily give up his way of life.

Wanting to live, he was making preparations to die. He wrote a will and made Velma the sole benefactor of the estate, but he had other possessions that he wanted to personally give to recipients. Guns. He always had a collection, including rifles and shotguns of various makes and calibers and gauges, appropriate for a man who enjoyed hunting. He also had guns that had sentimental value, including the first .22 rifle he had purchased as a teenager, ordered through the Gascozark Store. There was also the single-shot twelve-gauge shotgun that had been his father's. David had built a lockable gun rack for him in high school shop class, and that was where the guns were stored. As death neared, in an act that was more ritualistic than anything else, Ralph selected a gun for each male member of the family, including his son-in-law.

In her January 5, 1989, weekly community column in the *Richland Mirror*, correspondent May Hulsey noted that "Velma and Ralph hosted Xmas dinner for several family members." Velma had indeed prepared a fine meal and several were invited. But it was to be the last Christmas dinner celebration at which Ralph would be present. Before the arrival of the next yule time, the cancer would have taken its ultimate toll.

Any further hope that the tumor might shrink, never to return, finally vanished. The final phase of the ordeal started in early December when Ralph and Eddie briefly went out hunting and the ailing man was confined to the vehicle. This would be his last hunt, for the next day he complained of intense pain in his back.

When Ralph was admitted to St. John's Hospital in Springfield, a second tumor was discovered. Options were discussed, none of them hopeful, all of them leading to the same conclusion. Ralph chose comfort measures only and with his increasing paralysis, the doctors warned that he would surely die within weeks. For a short time, when it seemed he might be able to go home for his final days, plans were being made for home care. That plan was dropped shortly afterwards when he experienced a marked decline. Family members were alerted, and all the immediate family gathered at the hospital to await the final scene, taking turns at his bedside, much as he had done so many times for others.

Then, in the final hour of his life, after being unconscious for days, something unusual happened. Ralph briefly rallied, seemed alert and fully aware of those present and his circumstances. He was able to speak a few words. To Cora, who was taking her turn at his bedside, he said, "I am doing to die soon. Take care of Mom." He lost consciousness and later revived again. This time, in a very weak voice, he said, "I am going to die soon. Gather the family." These words were spoken without emotion, in a quiet, almost businesslike tone. It was as though in his dying, he wanted to manage that small bit of life in which he could exert some control.

Soon the family filled the room, assembling around the bed. He asked that the oxygen mask be removed, and then continued in a low, calm, and strangely directive voice.

"I love you and will see you on the other side."

Those were his last words, as he then took several long, increasingly deep breaths, and a few minutes later, stopped breathing altogether.

Ralph may have experienced what end-of-life researchers have termed "terminal lucidity," as described by Sara Manning Peskin, MD. This period of mental clarity and awareness just before death is a known phenomenon, though the exception rather than the rule.[78] Whatever the explanation for his clarity after many hours in a coma-like state, it helped the family better deal with his dying.

Among the assembled family, the hard grief of losing someone they loved was deeply felt, but with Ralph's passing, a profound sense of love seemed to envelop the room. Ralph's last moments had been filled with calm. If fears of the unknown lingered, he did not reveal them. There were those last few reassuring comments, then, satisfied that he had said all that needed to be said, he left the room. There was something in his words, his serenity, his assurances that provided for those present a sense of the rightness of his death, despite the accompanying feelings of grief and loss. It was as though he had somehow made it seem okay that he was dying, an effort that eased other members of the family as they contemplated their own deaths.

The return home that night in the darkness, as the family left the body of husband and father back at the hospital, was sorrowful. Coming into the driveway, the appearance of his truck, the white Ford Ralph purchased at retirement, was a sad reminder that he would not be using it again. At Velma's request, the truck was moved out of sight the next day and later sold.

Grief stricken, Velma was also realistic. As always, she was the accepter of hard realities. Ralph had told Cora there was plenty of money and to make sure Velma used it, but the truth was their savings were modest and Ralph had failed to calculate the cost of his own funeral. After making funeral arrangements and eyeing the hefty bill, Velma remarked, "Well, that about wipes me out." She would go on to manage more than well enough, although she saw clearly that her financial situation had changed and that she would have to move forward without the financial and practical assistance of her husband.

The day of Ralph's funeral was sunny, but that winter turned out to be one of the worst ever for the region, with lots of snow and frigid temperatures. According to the weather bureau, December 1989 was one of the coldest on record for that part of the Ozarks. Cold temperatures combined with wind created many days of bitter chill as the temperatures fell well into the double digits below zero.

There was snow on the ground, with many roads still slick, but Cora had invited Velma to her home in Blue Springs for the holiday. On Christmas Day it was a slow, cautious drive to Blue Springs on roads still partially covered with snow and icy in some spots. It was a sad, understated Christmas in many respects, but Velma was in no mood to do any celebrating in her own home, and she welcomed the opportunity to leave the house for a time and be with her family on that first Christmas without her spouse of more than fifty years.

THE WIDOW

THE CHILDREN RALLIED around their mother, offering time, transportation, and whatever practical assistance was needed. Friends and relatives provided words of comfort as well. Despite all that, the hard reality was that Velma was alone, and loneliness was to become one of her greatest challenges.

In March, a few months after Ralph's death, she wrote Don describing her gratitude at the help she was getting from "the boys" with some repairs around the house. She expressed pleasure at the recent visit from Cora and Todd, but added that it was "lonesome when they left." She had just printed flyers for the sale of Ralph's tools and fishing equipment, admitting that it was "not easy to see Dads things go but no good for me and that is what he would want me to do."

She struggled to keep the supplemental wood stove going, a job that had been previously assigned to Ralph, and she had concerns about the cost of wood and gas. Summing up that period of her life, she wrote, "It's been a job but a person can do lots of things if they have to." That was Velma to the core. Now, as throughout her life, she would do whatever needed to be done. If someone tried to be supportive and went on too long about her loss and circumstances, she would reply, "It's just life." Saying that was not an effort to dismiss the deep impact of her loss, but rather a true rendition of her living philosophy. One carried on and did the best they could with whatever they had, no matter what.

After over fifty years of marriage she was learning to be single, and it was difficult. She continued to be deeply appreciative of her children, realizing that she was now in many ways dependent upon them. That was true as far as transportation was concerned. Carl, who of the five children lived closest, regularly took her shopping, for which she was not only grateful but also insistent on giving him a few dollars for gas, something he neither expected nor wanted. Velma said, "I always give him money for gas. I don't sponge with no one." She was reluctant to ask her sister next door for transportation, as Cora often preferred to run errands alone. Velma felt like she was being intrusive just by asking. There was the church bus, but she did not like to take that either. Going to church alone was not the same, and taking the bus was a visible sign of her undesired status as a widow, alone, who needed help. The church and religion in general had never had the same meaning for her as it had for Ralph. For him religion was an ongoing search to dig into scriptural passages, to glean further understanding, and to pray for guidance. Velma, on the other hand, viewed the church as part of the greater framework of her life. It was a given, a broad general tradition she did not question, but her focus was on the practical points and particularly the relationships involved in everyday living.

When the couple first moved back to Hazelgreen in preparation for Ralph's retirement, Velma was determined to become more independent and to learn to drive, a sensible skill for anyone, especially one living in a rural area where there were no public alternatives. Ralph had been less than supportive of her goal, perhaps because he was comfortable with their long-standing dynamic and not eager to see it changed. He did start to instruct her, but he was an impatient teacher of basic skills. Carl took over as instructor and she progressed enough after several weeks to take the driving test. The written part went well enough, but the driving portion was a complete failure, devastating her plans. Once she stepped into the car with the DMV official who would judge and evaluate her actual driving, she became so anxious she could not perform what she had learned and she was unable to complete the test. She returned home frustrated, disappointed in herself, so much so that she completely gave up that particular quest for independence. But the lack of that skill would make its full impact once she became a widow years later.

Houseplants, flowers, and crafts had always been of interest, and she continued to work on projects, but with less enthusiasm. Television reception, even with a large outside antenna, was often poor, even for the two or three local channels she was able to pick up. Family members arranged to have a satellite dish installed, and the new device did bring in many more channels, but she watched only occasionally, and more often than not she fell asleep in her chair. Television was no substitute for a living presence. "No one knows how lonely it is all alone," she wrote.

There were ways in which, despite loss and loneliness, Velma blossomed during that period of her life. She took pride in initiating a number of long-overdue repairs on the house. She sold the car and converted the covered driveway into a screened porch on which she enjoyed sitting and listening to the sounds of the katydid and frogs. Doing so could make her feel lonely, yet, in another way, she was comforted by those familiar sounds. She continued to look for ways to keep busy, to occupy her time. She no longer had much interest in cooking, just for herself, but still made special treats, such as chocolate pie, for visitors. She took pleasure in being able to do more things for herself as she was now completely in charge of household matters. Her income from social security, although reduced with Ralph's death, provided adequately for her needs, with enough left over to maintain a growing savings account.

As Ralph had understood, Velma did enjoy traveling and would have done much more had her spouse been so inclined. In 1972, accompanied by her daughter Cora, she had made a trip to Santa Rosa, California, to visit Verga. In good health at that time, she, Verga, and Cora Hake had squeezed into Don's tiny Volkswagen and driven to Lindsay, California, for a visit with Cora and Lewis Posten.

Now, as a widow, Velma took more trips. Once she flew to San Francisco with Cora and Don and made another visit to Santa Rosa to visit Verga, who was now living in an assisted living facility. At a later time she flew unaccompanied to Portland to visit Don. During both trips she enjoyed the ocean and would calmly sit for some time, just looking out at the incoming tide or walking on the shore picking up stones.

On a side trip to Mendocino, California, she again appreciated the sea and the many sights there, including the house that served as the set for the home of Jessica Fletcher, the fictional sleuth in the television series *Murder She Wrote*, which she sometimes watched. By the time she took yet another trip to Portland to visit Don and his partner, Timothy, her mobility had declined considerably and she needed the support of a cane. It took considerable courage for her to board that plane alone and make the solo trip. She relished the experience, and felt better about life because of it. May Hulsey's newspaper column in July of 1996 reported that Velma had just returned from Oregon and that "She had the most wonderful time she had had in a long time." She later commented that the trip had been like a dream.

Velma enjoyed relatively good health over the years but experienced her share of ailments, some of which were related to aging. She was born with one leg shorter than the other and as a youth had worn a shoe with an elevated heel. In later life she had back problems that once required surgery, ineffective though it was. Back issues would continue to plague her. In May of 1978, when she was around sixty years of age, May Hulsey reported in her column that "Velma Posten hasn't been feeling too good this week. She is having trouble with her back." There were other body pains as well, and they became more pronounced over time. "The pain is not pleasant. Hard for me to walk," Velma wrote, and in the same letter expressed one more time how grateful she was for the help of her children.

In the spring of 1995 she was admitted to St. John's Hospital in Springfield in critical condition after suffering a ruptured appendix. For a time her very survival was at risk. The rupture had occurred at home days earlier, but she had told no one of the pain, revealing the problem only when it became clear she was not getting any better and needed to see a doctor. Fortunately, the medical team was able to successfully treat the problem and she soon returned to her home.

Velma grieved over the declining health of her sister Cora, who was now confined to a care center, and she worried about the health of her only brother, as well as other relatives and friends. Those who had been closest to her had died or were ailing. She was now clearly worried about her own future as well. "I know this is going to have to change but don't know what, I don't even get to go anywhere. I can't walk to shop now, hope can later. I use walker and cane," she wrote. She was struggling and family members worked with her toward a solution that seemed impossible to find. Suggestions that she sell the house and move to town nearer to one of the children went nowhere. She appreciated the attempts to help but dismissed them outright. "What would I do in Blue Springs?" she asked rhetorically when the subject of living near her daughter Cora came up. She could not envision a better life elsewhere, despite the obvious problems of her current living situation. Whatever life was to offer her in her final years, and she had reason to believe the outlook was gloomy, full of more loneliness and limitations in mobility, she judged that at least in her own home, in her own familiar surroundings, she could live life on her own terms.

It was difficult to see Velma struggling at times in her lonely life in the country, knowing that no number of visits or offers of help would resolve the problem. Circumstances beyond her control had left her a widow, without transportation, ill, with limited mobility, living on a rural road. But it was her own character, a sense of person and place, that resisted change and kept her there.

Her own mother had faced similar and yet different circumstances in her old age. Nora had reached a critical stage where she declared the living situation must change, a move was necessary. Velma never reached that point. There were a lot of negative aspects to her life, and positive ones as well, but her decision to stay put may have been partially based on her feeling that a physical move was no guarantee of contentment.

As the years rolled by and she suffered more losses, including the death of her beloved sister, Verga, her sense of loneliness grew more profound. In her last year, her diabetes was not well controlled. At one point she had to be hospitalized. There was some confusion about her medications, and it was clear she was not eating well; she received no satisfaction in preparing meals for herself. A crisis was in the making.

ANOTHER DEATH

THE NIGHT OF December 15, 1998, was not only the critical turning point for Velma, but also a difficult, anxious, and challenging one for those who loved her. Her health was failing and she was weak, reporting back pain. The family had begun to understand that she was no longer able to manage her care, and living on her own was no longer a reasonable option. Assisted living and nursing home care were being considered. There was certain to be a difficult conversation with their mother who, despite the issues, still had a definite preference to live independently. That conversation could wait, though, as a definitive diagnosis of her current condition had not been made. Velma was already dying, but no one could know that.

Cora left her job in Blue Springs on December 15 to come and stay a few days with her mother, anticipating a visit to the hospital for comprehensive testing the following day. On that fateful evening David was also present, but he left around nine, as Cora was spending the night and there was no observable evidence of an impending crisis.

As the evening wore on, Velma became more ill. Cora, in an effort to prepare her mother for the medical appointment, noticed a bright red spot the size of a strawberry on her chest.

Concerned, she asked if she had fallen, and was told no, she had not. Later, Cora saw foul-smelling blood in the commode, and she became seriously worried. Velma refused to eat anything and when it was suggested she might die if she did not eat, the feeble reply was, "That would be okay." In a telephone call to Don that evening, Velma could only mumble, barely audible, in a weak, distressed voice.

Immediate medical attention was needed. Cora called Eddie and they called an ambulance. When the EMTs arrived, they checked Velma's vital signs and reported that they were all normal. Velma seemed coherent, they said, and since she was complaining about her back, they were concerned about causing injury if they tried to carry her through the doorway on a gurney. They declined to transport her to the hospital. Frustrated, worried, and angered, Cora helped her mother into the rear seat of Eddie's car and drove her to the Lake Hospital. Once in the car, Velma could barely speak. "Why did they put me off so long?" she asked. Those were the last words she spoke. At the hospital they had time only to tell their mother they loved her as she was wheeled back into the emergency room. Several anxious minutes later a nurse returned to say, "I am sorry, we lost her."

Velma's death on December 16, 1998, came just one week after the death of her brother, Lewis. Her sister, Cora, would live another three years in a nursing home and die in February of 2001. Cora's death marked the end of a generation. Now all the children of Mart and Phoebe Posten, as well as those of Carl and Nora Clark, had died.

But there were still more stories to be told, as the children of Ralph and Velma realized that they were now, without question, the older generation—at the top of the list, next in line.

EPILOGUE

It was a beautiful fall day at the Hazelgreen Cemetery, graced by moderate temperatures, blue skies, and a hint of color in the surrounding timber. The familiar and strangely comforting hum of traffic on I-44 just across from the silence of old Rt. 66 played in the background. If their beloved Aunt Ella were still alive, she might have commented as she was known to have done, that it was a beautiful day for a funeral. Happily, on this particular autumn day, members of the Posten family, many years after the deaths of both parents, had come not to grieve at the passing of another loved one but instead to meet with Elvis Ogle, president of the Hazelgreen Cemetery Board, to select their own plots, which they hoped not to utilize until sometime in the distant future.

Although this was where so many of the family's burials had taken place, and was filled with gravestones bearing the names of Posten and Clark as well as a host of other relatives and friends, and despite the fact that what they were doing that day was a sharp unqualified reminder of their own mortality, the mood was light, even jovial.

Elvis carried with him a large three-ring notebook filled with handwritten pages depicting the various plots and their owners. He reminded the family that many plots had been laid out incorrectly over the years, resulting in wasted space within the limited cemetery grounds.

His voluntary job, once performed by their own father, Ralph, was to keep all that information and assure that future plots were assigned correctly. It was clear that cemetery management required skillful planning and was open to plenty of criticism from the public.

The location of desired plots was discussed. The idea was to be buried in the general area where generations of Postens and Clarks were loosely grouped. The available ground just south of Ralph and Velma's monuments was passed over by a makeshift road that crisscrossed its way across the cemetery, and the idea of a road passing over their graves did not sit well, although Elvis argued persuasively that what they saw was not really a road, but merely a temporary passageway that could be easily corrected. There were vacant plots to the east, directly across from their parents. In the end they selected locations to the east and to the south, their qualms about a road running through the area appeased by Elvis's reassurances.

Their work done, the children of Ralph and Velma Posten said their farewells and departed from the silent graves of their ancestors, back to their own busy routines, where they would create more stories in this never-ending family saga.

NOTES

1. Francis Parkman Jr. *The Oregon Trail.* "The Frontier." 1846.

2. History of Pulaski County. "Richland." First Edition. The Pulaski County Historical Society. 1982.: 88-89.

3. Elizah Baldwin Huntington. *History of Stamford, Connecticut.* From the Settlement in 1641 to the present time. Published by the author. 1868:10.

4. Clark, Edgar W. Rev. History and Genealogy of Samuel Clark Sr. and His Descendants from 1636-1891. Nixon-Jones Printing Co. St. Louis, Mo: July 1891.

5. Robert Lincoln Barlow. "Diary." June 27, 1891 to January 13,1904: January 1 and 11, 1901.

6. "John Ewing. Shawnee Indian Captivtie." Various accounts of the Capture of John Ewing. Submitted by Mary Hill. http://wwwusgennet.lrg/usa/ga/topic/ Indian/John Ewing. Ancestry.com.

7. George Matthews. At the dictation of Gen. A.T. Holcomb. "Clendenin Massacre." *West Virginia Historical Magazine.* 1904.

8. John T. Flynn. quoted in. *God's Gold. The Story of*

Rockefeller and his Times. New York. Brance and Co. 1904:211–212.

9. Ron Chernow. Quoted in. *The Life of John D. Rockefeller Sr.* Random House. New York. 1998: 134.

10. Flynn: 211–212.

11. Ida Tarbell. *The History of Standard Oil.* 1904. Briefer version edited by David M. Chambers. Dover Publications, Inc. Mineola, New York. 1966.

12. Henry Demarest Lloyd." The Story of a Great Monopoly." *Atlantic Monthly.* 1881.

13. Flynn: 165–166.

14. Matthew Josephson. *The Robber Barons. The Great American Capitalists. 1861–1901.* 1934. Harcourt Publishers. Published by Tranaction Publishers. New Brunswick USA and London. 2011: viii.

15. Flynn: 20–22.

16. Chernow: 153.

17. "Funeral of Jabez A. Bostwick," *The New York Times.* August 20, 1892.

18. "J.A. Bostwick's Sudden End." *New York Tribune.* August 18, 1892.

19. "Funeral of Jabez A. Bostwick. *New York Times.* August 20. 1892.

20. Daytonia in Manhattan. "The Lost Bostwick Mansions." Web source.

21. Henry Anton Bostwick. *The Descendants of Arthur Bostwick of Stratford, Connecticut.* New York. 1901:321,370.

22. Bostwick. quoted in: 114.

23. "Frisbee House." Delaware County Historical Association. Web Source.

24. Frisbee House. Web source.

25. Frisbee House. Web source.

26. David L. Valuska and Christian B. Keller, with contributions by Scott Hartwig and Martin Oefele. *Damn Dutch: Pennsylvania Germans and Gettysburg.* Stackpole Books. Merchanicsburg, Pennsylvania. 2004. Kindle Edition: 107222–2226.

27. German Myth 7. "The Pennsylvania Dutch". about com. web resource.

28. Valuska and Keller. Kindle Edition: 3575.

29. Charles A. Whiteshot. *The Oil-Well Driller. A History of the World's Greatest Enterprise. The Oil Industry.* West Virginia. 1905:379.

30. Jane Ockershausen. Quoting J.H. Bone. "The Valley that Changed the World. Visiting the Drake Well Museum". *Pennsylvania Heritage Magazine.* Vol. XXI. NO. 3. Summer 1995. Reprinted Pennsylvania Heritage. Web Source.

31. William Marvel. "A Poor Man's Fight. The Civil War Common Soldier." National Park Service. U.S. Department of the Interior. Web Source.

32. Rebecca Onion. "The Man Who Fought in Lincoln's Name." The Volt. Web Source.

33. Robert Laird Stewart. *History of the One Hundred and Fortieth Regiment Pennsylvania Volunteers.* Published by the authority of the Regimental Association. Copyright William S. Shallenberger. 1912: 9

34. Stewart: 8.

35. Stewart: 15.

36. "A Description of the Battlefield at Gettysburg." *Daily*

Patriot and Union. July 11, 1863, Posted by Jake Wynn, July 10,2013. Web source.

37. Stewart. Thanksgiving Day. 1864.

38. Stewart. Quoted by: 249.

39. Dr. A.H. Acheson. *History of the One Hundred and Fortieth: Siege of Petersburgh*. By the authority of the Regimental Association: 68.

40. Stewart: 243.

41. *History of Pulaski County*. Southern Heritage Press. January 1, 1889: 89

42. Milton D. Rafferty. *The Ozarks Land and Life*. Second edition. "Settlements: The Later Stages." The University of Arkansas Press. Fayetteville. 2001: 62.

43. "Civil War Comes to Pulaski County." *Old Settlers Gazette*. The Stagecoach Stop Foundation. Issue 30-July 28,2012: 32

44. Steven D. Smith. *Made in the Timber: A Settlement History of the Fort Leonard Wood Region*. With contributions by Alex Prime. Library of Congress. 101 Independence Ave. SE. Washington, D.C.: 2003:64.

45. "Calloway Manes Killed by Bushwhackers." *Old Settlers Gazette*. The Old Stagecoach Stop Foundation. Editors. Jan and Terry Primas. July 28, 2012: 41.

46. Smith: 77–79.

47. Steven L. Damaree. "Post Civil War Immigration to Southwest Missouri 1865–1873. *Missouri Historical Review*. Vol. 69. 1975: 173.

48. Damaree: 175.

49. Smith: 116.

50. "The Lighter Side of the Ozarks," The Scoop. *The Lebanon Missouri Daily Record*. October 12, 1988.

51. *History of Pulaski County Missouri.* Vol. 1. 1982. Pulaski County Historical Society: 88–89.
52. Lawrence and Eula V. York. *Forty-'Leven Stories about Forty-'Leven People.* Western Publishing Co. Republic, Missouri. 1975: 136.
53. "Bloodland." Wikipedia.
54. York and York: 179.
55. *History of Pulaski County Missouri.* Vol. II. Pulaski County Historical Society. 1987: 138.
56. *History of Pulaski County, Missouri.* Southern Heritage Press. 1889: 140.
57. Tiley, Nannie M. editor, *Federals on the Frontier: The Diary of Benjamin F. McIntyre, 1862–1864.* Austin, University of Texas Press. 1963: 14 Quoted by Steven D. Smith, *Made in the Timber: 55–56.*
58. Diary of Lyman G. Bennett. Quoted by Steven D. Smith: 56.
59. *History of Pulaski County. 1889:* 120.
60. York and York. *Forty-Leven Stories: 81–82.*
61. Oma Willits Hensley. *Early Churches of Pulaski County.* 1970. Missouri Baptist Press. Jefferson City, Missouri: 193.
62. Robert Lincoln Barlow. "Diary". June 27 1891-January 13, 1904: Sept. 30, 1893.
63. Barlow: February 22, 1892.
64. Barlow: January 3, 1895.
65. Mabel Manes Mottaz. BS.MA. *Lest We Forget. A History of Pulaski County Missouri and Fort Leonard Wood.* 1960:33.
66. Carl O. Sauer. *The Geography of the Ozark Highland of Missouri.* University of Chicago Press. January. 1927: 1.

67. Smith: 174.

68. *History of Pulaski County Missouri.* "History of Fairview Baptist Church." Vol. II. 1987, Pulaski County Historical Society: 45.

69. Willits: 196.

70. Willits: 157–158.

71. Robert K. Gilmore. "The Church as Entertainment." *Ozark Watch.* Vol. V. No. 3. Winter 1992. Article adapted from *Ozark Baptizings, Hangings, and other Diversions.* University of Oklahoma Press.

72. *History of Pulaski County.* Vol. II. 1987: 28.

73. Conor Watkins. *Ozark Mountain Experience.* Articles 23 and 24 combined. "Devil's Elbow, Clifty Creek, and Lane Spring." Web site. www.rollannet.org.

74. Augusta Howlett Black. *All In The Name of Love.* Copy located in Genealogy Room. Pulaski County Library, Richland, Missouri. 1977: 2.

75. Smith: 156–159.

76. "Frank A. Jones and Gascozark." *Old Settlers Gazette.* The Old Stagecoach Foundation. 2007: 46.

77. Christina Crapanzano. "A Brief History of Rt. 66." *Time Magazine.* June 28, 2010.

78. Sarah Manning Peskin, MD. "The Gentler Symptoms of Dying." *New York Times.* July 11, 2017.

BIBLIOGRAPHY

"Accidental Shooting is Fatal." <u>The Richland Mirror.</u> Richland, Missouri: March 1961.

Acheson, Dr. A.H. <u>History of the One Hundred and Fortieth.</u> Siege of Petersburgh. By the Authority of the Regimental Association: :Philadelphia:1912.

Barlow, Robert Lincoln. <u>Diary.</u> June 27, 1891 to January 13, 1904. Tape recorded and translated by Bonnie Elam McIntyre and Dr Flora Elam Lawrence, Daughters of Joe and Nettie Elam, grand daughters of Eliza Ann Barlow Elam. Effie Barlow Chamberlin 1983.

Printed by Robert E. Parkin, Research Productions, 6611 Clayton Rd. St. Louis, Mo Copy located in the Genealogy Room of Pulaski County Library, Richland, Missouri.

Black, Augusta Howlett. <u>All in the Name of Love</u>. :1977. Copy located in Genealogy Room, County Library, Richland, Missouri.

Bostwick, Henry Anton. <u>The Descendants of Arthur Bostwick of Stratford, Connecticut.</u>New York: 1901.

Chernow, Ron. The Life of John D. Rockefeller Sr. Random House. New York : 1998.

Clark, Edgar W. Rev. History and Genealogy of Samuel Clark Sr. and His Descendants from 1636-1891. Nixon-Jones Printing Co. St. Louis, Mo: July 1891.

Crapanzano, Christina. "A Brief History of Rt. 66." Time Magazine.:June 28, 2010.

Damaree, Steven L. "Post Civil War Immigration to Southwest Missouri 1865-1873." Missouri Historical Review. Vol.69.1975.

"Daytonia in Manhattan: The Lost Bostwick Mansions-NOS 800-801 5th Ave." The stories behind the buildings, statues, and other points of interest that made Manhattan fascinating. Web based Blog.:January 7, 2013.

Duerden, Tim. "A History of the Frisbee House." Delaware County Historical Association. Web. source.

Flynn, John T. God's Gold the Story of Rockefeller and his Times. New York: Brance and Co: 1904.

"Frank A. Jones and Gascozark." Old Settlers Gazette: The Old Stagecoach Foundation: 2007.

"Frisbee Haunted House." Web source.

Frisbee House. George Gideon. Wikipedia.

"Funeral of Jabez A. Bostwick." New York Times. New York, New York.:August 20, 1892.

"Funeral of Mr. Bostwick," The Sun. New York, New York.: August 20, 1892.

"German Language, German Misnomers, Myths and Mistakes. Myth 7. The Pennsylvania Dutch." Web source. about.com.

Giddens, Paul H. The Birth of the Oil Industry. New York: The MacMillan Co: 1938.

Gilbert, Joan. The Trail of Tears Across Missouri. University of Missouri Press. Columbia, Missouri: 1996. The Curators of the University of Missouri.

Gilmore, Robert K. "The Church as Entertainment." Ozark Watch. Vol. V. No. 3: Winter 1992. Article adapted from Ozark Baptizings, Hangings, and other Diversions. University of Oklahoma Press.

Gourley, Bruce. "Baptist and the American Civil War." Macron Telegraph: February 7, 1861.

Hicks, Emma Page. "Early History of Pioneer Pulaski County, Missouri." Articles written by Emma Page Hicks. Published in the Pulaski County Democrat, and The Daily Guide, between 1977 and 1983. Tituville, Florida. Privately Published by Donald W. Page. Volumns 1,2,3. 1994.

Hidy, Ralph W. and Muriel E. Pioneering in Big Business 1882-1911. Harper and Brothers.

New York: Copyright by the Business History Foundation Inc:1955.

Hill, Mary. "Various Accounts of the Capture of John Ewing." ancestry.com

History of Pulaski County Missouri. Southern Heritage Press.:January 1, 1889.

History of Pulaski County Missouri. Vol. 1, Pulaski County Historical Association. Waynesville, Missouri: 1982..

History of Pulaski County Missouri. Vol. 2. Pulaski County Historical Society. Waynesville, Missouri:1987.

History of Stratford, Connecticut: 1639-1939. Provo, Ut. The Generations Network Inc. 2005. Original Data, William Howard Wilcoxson. History of Stratford, Connecticut 1639-1939. Stratford Tercentenary Commission. 1939. Web source.

Hulsey, Mae. "Hazelgreen Items." The Richland Mirror. Vol. 68. Richland, Missouri; January 19, 1978.

Hulsey,. "Hazelgreen Items.": January 5, 1989.

Hulsey, Mae. "Hazelgreen Items." :July 11, 1996.

Huntington, Elizah Baldwin. History of Stamford, Connecticut. From the Settlement in 1641 to the present time. Published by the author.:1868.

"Indian John Ewing." West Virginia Archives and History. ancestry.com.

"J.A. Bostwick's Sudden End." New York Tribune. New York, New York.:August 18, 1892.

"John Ewing and the Clendenin Massacre." West Virginia Archives and History. West Virginia Historical Magazine:1904. From an original sketch by George P. Matthews at the dictation of General A. T. Holcomb. 1803-1877.

Josephson, Matthew. The Robber Barons. The Great American Capitalists.1861-1901.(1934) Tranaction Publishers. New Brunswick USA and London: 2011. Originally published by Harcourt.

Kerchner, Charles F. "Pennsylvania Dutch are of German Heritage. Not Dutch."Emaus, Pennsylvania: 1966.

Lloyd, Henry Demarest. "Story of a Great Monopoly." The Atlantic Monthly:1881.

Marvel, William. "A Poor Man's Fight. The Civil War Common Soldier." National Park Service. U.S. Department of the Interior.

Mottaz, Mabel Manes BS, MA. Lest We Forget A History of Pulaski County Missouri and Fort Leonard Wood . Cain Printing Co. Springfield:1960.

Ockershausen, Jane. "The Valley that Changed the World: Visiting the Drake Museum." Vol. XXL. No.3. Summer 1995 Pennsylvania State Historic Preservation Office. Quoting an article by J.H. Bone, a reporter for the Cleveland, Ohio Herald. Petroleum Wells. (1865).

"Civil War Commemorative Issue. "Old Settlers Gazette." The Old Stagecoach Stop Foundation. Pulaski County, Missouri. Issue 30,:July 28, 2012.

Onion, Rebecca. "The Man Who Fought in Lincoln's Name." The Volt. Web source.

Parkman, Francis. The Oregon Trail: 1847.

Parsons, Olive. "The Lighter Side of the Ozarks" The Scoop. Lebanon Daily Record. Lebanon, Missouri,:October 12, 1988.

Pearche, Kirp. "Hazelgreen was Early County Town." Article on Display at Rt. 66 Museum, Lebanon, Missouri.

Peskin, Sara Manning MD. "The Gentler Symptoms of Dying". N.Y. Times,:July 11, 2017.

Rafferty, Milton. The Ozarks: Land and Life. Second Edition. The University of Arkansas Press. Fayetteville;2001.

Sauer, Carl O. The Geography of the Ozark Highland of Missouri. University of Chicago Press: January, 1927.

Smith, Steven D. "A Historic Context Statement for a World War II ERA Black Officer's Club at Ft. Leonard Wood, Missouri. " US Department of Defense Legacy Resource Management. Champaign, Illinois and Columbia, South Carolina. US Army Construction Engineering Research Laboratories and the South Carolina Institute of Archaeology.

Smith,Steven D. Made in the Timber: A Settlement History of the Fort Leonard Wood Region. With contributions by Alex Prime. Library of Congress. 101 Independence Ave. SE Washington DC.: 2003.

Stewart, Robert Laird, DD. History of the One Hundred and Fortieth Regiment Pennsylvania Volunteers. Published by the authority of the Regimental Association. Copyright William S. Shallenberger: 1912.

Tarbell, Ida. The History of Standard Oil. 1904. Briefer version edited by David M. Chambers. Dover Publications, Inc. Mineola, New York: 1966. Original Publication by Macmillan Co.

Valuska, David L. and Christian B, Keller, with contributions by Scott Hartwig and Martin Oefele. Damn Dutch: Pennsylvania Germans at Gettysburg. Stackpole Books. Mechanicsburg, Pennsylvania:2004. 2010.

Watkins, Conor. "Ozark Mountain Experience." Articles 23 and 24 Combined. Devils's Elbow, Cliffy Creek, and Lane Spring. Website. www.rollannet.org.

Weinberg, Steve. Taking on the Trust. The Epic Battle of Ida Tarbell and John D. Rockefeller.

WW Norton and Company. New York. London: 2008.

Whiteshot, Charles A. <u>The Oil Driller. A History of the World's Greatest Enterprise; The Oil Industry.</u> West Virginia: 1905.

Willits, Oma Hensley. <u>Early Churches of Pulaski County.</u> Missouri Baptist Press:1970.

York, Laurence, and Eula V. York. <u>Forty-'Leven Stories about Forty-'Leven People.</u> Republic, Missouri. Western Publishing Co: 1975.